GULF

OF

MEXICO

95°

90°

25°

TAMPICO

·54

55

VERACRUZ

41 ·18
7
·27
30

20°

MERIDA
○
·23   ·10
9·   ·15
8·   ·15   14·

Yucatan

44
29 36
33· 12 ·13
32 ·45
53

Chiapas

3

4
·38

7

5   2
·1

6

British
Honduras

Guatemala

·17

15°

MAP BY: H.L. BERNSTEIN

95°

90°

STYLE IN MEXICAN ARCHITECTURE

STYLE IN MEXICAN ARCHITECTURE

By RICHARD ALDRICH

Photographs by
MERLE G. WACHTER *and*
RICHARD MERRICK

Coral Gables, Florida:

UNIVERSITY OF MIAMI PRESS

Copyright © 1968 by University of Miami Press
Library of Congress Catalog Card Number: 66-29910

Manufactured in the United States of America
Printed by Parker Printing, Coral Gables, Florida
Book and Jacket Design: Norman Baker Koski

In Memory of

Lorenzo Eugene Aldrich

Preface

A long time ago, in the midst of the Huerta phase of the Mexican Revolution, refugees used to take employment with the railroads operating in the American Southwest. In the camps at Wichita and around Liberal in southwestern Kansas I first saw these people. The men could work all day and, if there was moonlight, sing much of the night. They could sing in spite of the fact that most of their earnings were reclaimed for a regimen of malnutrition at the commissary car. Some money changed hands in gambling in the empty box-car casino with watchers at the door. Inside, a paraffin candle laid a ring of light on the floor, and around it a circle of dark faces and glittering eyes pursued the game. At the right hand of an occasional player a stiletto was stuck in the floor. Outside, tight in black *rebozos* and dragging black skirts, the women tried to cook for their families in tomato cans over a handful of fire. This was my first sight of the world's underprivileged and oppressed; it was my first sight of things Mexican.

Years later, when I paid my first visit to their country, my surprise was so great that the excitement and interest of it lasted and now, after three decades, has grown. Brilliant, beautiful cities like Zacatecas and Oaxaca, built for people to live in, have an architecture that is related to life; fine sculpture, trees, flowers, parks, a living theatre; schools, teachers; a religion and its equipment that greatly deepens with its significance the whole outlook of the people. In addition to this, one has the experience of appraising a planned economy not without concepts to enrich its *laissez-faire.* All this, and more, is cheerfully, even gaily, borne side by side with something not far, sometimes, from malnutrition. It is no Calvinist crime to be poor in Mexico. It is the fate of many Christians who have all leave to "work their way out of it" if they will. They do not entertain the satanic alienation that we seem to have. They are alive, and such a life as they have can be trained at the top by traditional forces such as the Catholic faith of Mexico, its actual cultural matrix that bravely survived the difficulties of the Revolution.

This one has to go to Mexico to see, to apprehend. It is an easy matter to call to mind the few North American scholars who portray the veracity of the Mexican scene. Bolton and Kubler, McAndrew and some novelists can do this. But very many people writing historical studies have not forgotten the pernicious assumptions inherited from eighteenth century British historical works. These same assumptions are not avoided in anthropology. One such writer has expressed the regret that the *teocalli* no longer tops the hill. It seems not easy for them to remember the quality of those first Spaniards who came to further the fruits of grace. History seems to remember mostly the works of the exploiters. But the exploiters eventually suffer defeat. The idealism, no matter how deeply covered over, reasserts itself. And so the best that was attempted in the early sixteenth century comes out in the new life and laws after the Revolution.

In the future it is going to be necessary to appraise less generously the hordes of indrifting unknowns and their successors the Toltecs, the Chichimecs, the Tenocha-Aztecs, and others. For the great *temenos* at Teotihuacan now gives off, in the new excavations, more and more light. It is revealing the people of classic times whose return, in the forms of the spirit, breaks through the iron lava of the Aztec floration and its ways in the vulgarities of theocratic chicanery attributed to the Huitzilopochtli clergy. It almost seems that we like to think it is these destructive forces in history which are the ones that survive. Brilliant Texcoco sinks, and grim Tenochtitlan gains the power. But the good may rise again and grow, changed in its forms but not in its essence. It is this vision of the coming Mexico, rising out of the best of its Classic Age and out of the best great contributions of the Conquest, both outstandingly theocentric, that makes an awesome convergence to enter the culture's springtime of the next millennium. One comes to conclude that this convergence bears Mexico on a highway heading into an unfolding — renewed, heightened, exalted — to rise over the sordid times of its Jacobin interlude.

The present work rose out of an invitation to help with the tasks of training the lay apostolate at the Center for Intercultural Formation in Cuernavaca. Monsignor Ivan Illych wanted a series of pictures with informative legends. Then the original purpose was left behind. More background seemed to be called for, and in the expanding of the historical section, the work grew into the present more formal stage.

Such a work is the labor of many hands. Many of the photographs of the New Empire sites and of viceregal time were supplied by Professor Merle Wachter, Chairman of the Art Department at the University of the Americas (formerly Mexico City College). He enlarged and re-established my acquaintance with the art of Mexico in many ways. Through his courtesies I owe many thanks to the National Institute of Anthropology and History, where I made use of the photography archives. Dr. Ignacio Bernal, the Director of the National Museum of Anthropology, has been hospitable in Oaxaca, and generous with introductions.

After this work had been completed, there came to notice, once more, the distinguished work in photography of Professor Richard Merrick, in his distinction doyen indeed of the Department of Art of the University of Miami. This had been a matter of living too close to excellence to remember awareness of it. Some of the pictures in his photographic essay serve to balance with the necessarily heavily subjective nature of this account of art in Mexico. I think his picture of the altars in San Cayetano, La Valenciana, Guanajuato, are perhaps the best ever to be published so far.

Two scholarship grants, secured by Mr. Maurice Ferré, gave me sojourns in Mexico and Guatemala for study. It was at the request of the Editor of the University of Miami Press at that time, Mrs. Marjory Stoneman Douglas, that Dr. Leonard Muller, my chief at the University of Miami Summer Sessions in Oaxaca, has read this work and helped with good basic suggestions. At the same request Dr. Henry Field read it, and made possible, through recommendations, my first stay at Tikal in Guatemala at the University of Pennsylvania Museum site there. I was there able to strengthen my views of Mayan art in discussions with the scholar who knows most about it, the then Director, Dr. Edwin Shook.

Dr. Ione Stuessy Wright, Editor of the *Journal of Inter-American Studies,* acted as editor of this work for the University of Miami Press. For urbanity of outlook, courteous patience and guidance I am very much indebted to her. Since the first study trip to Mexico many years ago, a part of which she kindly attended, she has throughout all Mexican contacts helped with friendship and support. And in all things pertaining to these study trips, Dr. C. Doren Tharp (then Vice President of the University of Miami) gave us counsel and support.

There was much secretarial counsel needed. It was supplied by Mrs. Mary Hunt of Cardiff, California, and by Mrs. Peggy Seaton and Miss Jane Hollman of Miami who have, and not only once, put this manuscript in form for me.

There is, too, the forethought and courtesies that librarians often give, and I have much thanks to all the staff of the University of Miami Library, not least to Mr. George Rosner and to that treasure, Miss Rose Beck.

Scholars everywhere in Mexico were helpful. So were the kind townspeople of Oaxaca. Besides those people there were American residents, Sr. Canuto and Mrs. Jennie Gleesen, who had suggestions for our Summer Sessions, some of which have been carried out now by others on a national scale. There was Sr. Clarence de Lima and the López magnates, and the fine staff of the Oaxaca Archaeological Museum. There were many friends in Tlacolula; in Mitla there was the entire Hacienda Frissell; in Teotitlan del Valle the guild of the weavers. There were the staff members of the *zona arqueológica* everywhere. And, lastly, with his clergy and with the lay elders of the Basilica of the Most Precious Blood in Teotitlan del Valle, his Grace, The Most Reverend Dr. Don Fortunato Gómez, the Archbishop of Antequera.

Richard Aldrich

Casa San Lorenzo
The Vigil of St. Lawrence, 1967
Encinitas, California

Illustrations

Plates VI, VI-B, VI-C, VII-A, VII-B, XIX, XXII-A, XXVIII-A, XXXII, XXXII-A, XLII, XLIV-A, XLVII-A, XLVII-B, XLVII-C, LV, LV-A, LV-B, LV-C, LV-D, LVI, LVI-A, and LXII by Richard Merrick; all others by Merle G. Wachter.

Plate I   Santo Domingo Yanhuitlan, Oaxaca. Apse.
Plate II   Santiago Tlatelolco, Distrito Federal. Façade.
Plate III   Santiago Tlatelolco, Distrito Federal. Façade.
Plate IV   Santiago Tlatelolco, Distrito Federal. Façade.
Plate V   Santiago Tlatelolco, Distrito Federal. Side view.
Plate VI, VI-A   Santo Domingo Yanhuitlan, Oaxaca. Façade.
Plate VI-B   Santo Domingo Yanhuitlan, Oaxaca. Side view.
Plate VI-C   Santo Domingo Yanhuitlan, Oaxaca. Interior.
Plate VII   Santiago Cuilapan, Oaxaca. The Second Basilica.
Plate VII-A, B   Santiago Cuilapan, Oaxaca.
Plate VIII   San Francisco, Tepeaca, Puebla. Vaulting.
Plate IX   Ixmiquilpan, Hidalgo. Vault of transept crossing.
Plate X   A church near San Cristóbal de las Casas, Chiapas.
Plate XI   San Pablo Yuriria, Querétaro. Façade.
Plate XII   San Pablo Yuriria, Querétaro. Tower.
Plate XIII   San Pablo Yuriria, Querétaro. Front view.
Plate XIV   San Pablo Yuriria, Querétaro. Façade, plateresque detail.
Plate XV   San Pablo Yuriria, Querétaro. Façade detail.
Plate XVI   San Agustín Acolman, Mexico, Distrito Federal.
                 Façade detail.
Plate XVII   La Santisima, Mexico, Distrito Federal. Façade,
                 upper storeys.

Plate XVIII   Santa Prisca, Taxco, Guerrero. Façade, upper storeys.
Plate XIX   La Valenciana, Guanajuato, Guanajuato. Sacristy door.
Plate XX   Natividad de Nuestra Señora, Tepoztlan, Morelos. Façade, main doorway.
Plate XXI   San Miguel, *Posa del Atrio,* Huejotzingo, Puebla.
Plate XXII   San Miguel, Huejotzingo, Puebla. Tequitqui Cross.
Plate XXII-A   San Miguel, Huejotzingo, Puebla. High altar.
Plate XXIII   Tequitqui Cross at the *Parroquia* at the Basilica of Guadalupe, Distrito Federal.
Plate XXIV   Santiago, Tlatelolco, Distrito Federal. Entrance to school.
Plate XXV   San Nicolás Actopan, Hidalgo. Refectory vaulting.
Plate XXVI   San Agustín Acolman, Hidalgo. Fresco, black and white.
Plate XXVII   View of Oaxaca de Juárez (Antequera), Oaxaca, from Monte Albán.
Plate XXVIII   Santo Domingo Oaxaca, Oaxaca. Façade, central panel.
Plate XXVIII-A   Santo Domingo, Oaxaca, Oaxaca.
Plate XXIX   Santo Domingo, San Cristóbal de las Casas, Chiapas.
Plate XXX   Hacienda Chapel, Vista Hermosa, Morelos. Elementary *estipites.*
Plate XXXI   *Sagrario,* Metropolitana, Mexico, Distrito Federal. Churrigueresque *estipites.*
Plate XXXII   *Sagrario,* Metropolitana, Mexico, Distrito Federal. Façade doorway.
Plate XXXII-A   *Sagrario,* Metropolitana, Mexico, Distrito Federal.
Plate XXXIII   Santa Prisca, Taxco, Guerrero. Façade, left half.
Plate XXXIV   Santa Prisca, Taxco, Guerrero. Doorway.
Plate XXXV   San Francisco, Mexico, Distrito Federal. Lateral entrance.
Plate XXXVI   La Compañía, Guanajuato, Guanajuato. Façade.
Plate XXXVII   La Compañía, Guanajuato, Guanajuato. Façade.
Plate XXXVIII   San Martín Tepotzotlán, Mexico. Façade.
Plate XXXIX   San Martín Tepotzotlán, Mexico. Façade, upper storey.
Plate XL   Santo Domingo, Oaxaca. Main cloister and façade towers.
Plate XLI   Cathedral, Saltillo, Coahuila. Façade, regional baroque.
Plate XLII   Chapel, Tepeyac, above the Basilica at Guadalupe, Distrito Federal.
Plate XLIII   House in Querétaro, Querétaro.
Plate XLIV   Organ, Metropolitana, Mexico, Distrito Federal. *Coro,* altar end.
Plate XLIV-A   Metropolitana, Mexico, Distrito Federal. Detail of altar.
Plate XLV   Kabah, Yucatán. Puuc manner, façade.
Plate XLVI   Kabah, Yucatán. Puuc manner, section.
Plate XLVII   Mitla, Oaxaca. Main quadrangle, wall section.
Plate XLVII-A   Mitla, Oaxaca. Temple and church.
Plate XLVII-B, C   Mitla, Oaxaca. Temple, patterned tepics.
Plate XLVIII   An *artesonada* doorway.
Plate XLIX   San Francisco Huejotzingo, Puebla.
Plate L   La Valenciana, Guanajuato, Guanajuato. Altar, and sacristy door sculpture.
Plate LI   San Agustín Church, Salamanca, Querétaro. St. Ann altar panel, right side.
Plate LII   San Agustín Church, Salamanca, Querétaro. The Virgin of Guadalupe altar.
Plate LIII, LIV   San Agustín Church, Salamanca, Querétaro. St. Joseph altar, right side.
Plate LV   La Valenciana, Guanajuato, Guanajuato, San Cayetano, High Altar.
Plate LV-A   La Valenciana, Guanajuato, Guanajuato. San Cayetano, side altar.
Plate LV-B   La Valenciana, Guanajuato, Guanajuato. San Cayetano, side altar, upper middle section.
Plate LV-C   La Valenciana, Guanajuato, Guanajuato. San Cayetano, dome.
Plate LV-D   La Valenciana, Guanajuato, Guanajuato.
Plate LVI   The Palace of the Conde de Canal, San Miguel de Allende, Guanajuato. Side doorway.
Plate LVI-A   The Palace of the Conde de Canal, San Miguel de Allende, Guanajuato. Side doorway.
Plate LVII   La Milagrosa, Mexico, Distrito Federal.
Plate LVIII   La Milagrosa, Mexico, Distrito Federal.
Plate LIX   La Milagrosa, Mexico, Distrito Federal.
Plate LX   La Purísima, Monterrey, Nuevo León.
Plate LXI   El Sagrado Corazón, Colonia del Valle, Mexico, D.F.
Plate LXII   La Asunción Cathedral, Oaxaca.

12

STYLE IN MEXICAN ARCHITECTURE

MEXICO is the Holy Land of the New World. The outward modern symbol of this role is the crowned Patroness at Tepeyac Hill, at the shrine of the Virgin of Guadalupe. No other nation has been so honored as has Mexico in this plenitude of grace. The new basilica now being planned is only the latest of many dedications. In ancient times, and after the Conquest and up until today, the activities of religion in Mexico have a fascinating record.

Travelers returning from Anáhuac, the high valley of Central Mexico, keep long in their recollection one particular accomplishment of Mexican piety, its rich modes in church architecture. To many observers the religious architecture in Mexico is likely to be the one outstanding travel experience. For travelers who have been to other Latin American countries the opulence of this art in Mexico will likely be a shock. There is no preparation at all for this experience in Cuba, or Guatemala — except in retrospect in Antigua — in Honduras or El Salvador. Peru has many contemporary works, but the order of the experience is likely somewhat different than it is in Mexico. For in Mexico the post-Revolution youthful vigor of religious life endows the remains of the older religious establishment with its own aura. The woodcarvers and builders, working in the baroque style at the Carmel in San Luis Potosí, shouted with

1

laughter at the question of their having learned their crafts in a school. They were guildsmen, working away with apprentices, templates, and molds. What school!

And there are many more immediate incidental episodes of this piety that move the recollection with warmth. They bring to remembrance the courtesies and the kindness found, it seems, almost everywhere. Who repaired your car, stalled on the long lonely road, sometimes for no charges, sometimes for less than a token? Where did you go in Mexico where you were not received in a most cordial manner! There was the taxi driver who searched so long for an address in the maze off Insurgentes; the earnest little guide, a dedicated person indeed, who tried so hard to remember in English all the cultural stratification at Cholula. Hours were patiently spent in a long search for a key to a chapel, so that one could see in his basilica at Pátzcuaro the golden casket containing the heart of the great bishop, Vasco de Quiroga. One saw the primal faith that placed bits of stock fodder on the altar, so that the *Pneuma* should sanctify also the modern food of the Friends who were present at the Incarnation, the Ox and the Ass, along with the Sun and the Moon. And there was the gentle touching of sacramentals, like the processional painting, and other palladia in Teotitlán del Valle's Feast of the Most Precious Blood.

For many of the visitors to Mexico who may not readily at first apprehend the overwhelming *caritas* in Mexican religious feeling, there are lesser ways in which Mexican piety has asserted itself in phases and transformations, through all its cultures. In the classic culture of long ago, this lofty view was set forth in the exalted ar-

Plate I   Santo Domingo Yanhuitlan, Oaxaca. Apse.

chitecture at Teotihuacan, about which Ignacio Bernal so clearly tells us. In the barbarian cultures it strove so desperately to set forth the panorama of the last end of man, heaven and hell, death and damnation, a vast eschatological program of placation. And in the fusion with Iberian forms it speaks with serene assurance of the necessity and the ways of redemption.

Architecture grows through long tradition in pre-Cortesian and Iberian works in Mexico. Its history is made up of the impact of several cultures. Cultures carry out their possibilities in the making of forms and symbols in the growing phases of material and immaterial way. Art is the making of these things and the making of them well. Art makes things in all the early stages — the precultural and the prehistoric states of societies, too. But when a human group has started on its growth, it is soon not entirely in the same even early state in all of its elements. For its own purposes, it attains a state in culture when traits in one group combine with those of another. These combinations become directional forms in the development and they are, for the culture, the limiting form of the future. There what becomes the eventual shrine, the house-form, the state, the cult, its liturgies, the vast mnemotechnic literatures, the modes of family life, the tradition of techniques, are all in quite early times molded by what becomes itself a growth, the eventual myth.

In most societies, this entire history is set forth by the cult, its shrine form and the communicating symbols, not least those that are involved with the last end of man. The myth sets forth the creation and the end of the world, and it is only to ourselves that this seems to be two stories: the mundane order and the world of the

17

Plate II   Santiago Tlatelolco, Distrito Federal. Façade.

Gods. It is no small matter to the eventual power in the use of
symbols that the myth is clear in its accretions and the symbols
explicit. It is the tradition of the life that these symbols of the myth
are the matter of the whole.

Thus, for example, the use of symbols in sculpture in pre-Cortesian religion sets forth a conjuration derived from earlier magic
that relates the operation to the deity whose power has been invoked.[1] The conjuration worked so effectively in its own time, as art,
that it works a little for us, too, as a relic of the art of the past, of
which we can have but seldom the barest real judgment. It is not
really art for us, for art is a constellation of total associations that
is involved in the living process of the maker and his folk. This piece
of sculpture was an invoked convention, addressed to the God-
world, and was not considered as a personal expression. It is shallow
vanity to think, in such situations, of the universal appeal of art.

There is no universal appeal for art. Our later judgments come
from later associations. Thus we may go on to see that the great
symbolic God-forms of the late Aztecs, for example, are all above
what would be connotations of the natural to us. They have, like their
architecture, to do with the truth that is in power and its terror. They
do not recall forms that we are used to seeing, nor forms that we
are used to thinking about. Such craftsmen as are involved in the
work of the hierophant, the maker of the image of the Mother, Coatlicue, have never heard of the pedantic rationalism of Socrates

[1] Paul Westheim, *The Sculpture of Ancient Mexico* (New York: Doubleday &
Company, Inc., 1963), p. 12.

18

Plate III   Santiago Tlatelolco, Distrito Federal. Façade.

and Plato, that art follows nature. The Stagirite, it is true, had a
chance to say something about the great variety of the categories
of knowledge. But he was not moved by the might of intuition that
could imagine the vast Kailāsanātha temple at Elūrā, to evoke,
induce, and carve it out of the hill. This ability of managing such
a yogic intention is also knowledge. But he went to the Platonic
view, that the logical procedure of discursive thought is knowledge
in its valuable mode. According to this view, then, nature is a copy
of ideas in the manner of Platonic universals, and art, a copy of
nature, is thus an imitation of an imitation. Art thus encompasses
less thought and less reality than nature.[2] It would be difficult to
get farther from the truth about art, unless one were even more
openly following the delusion of objective reality.

The purpose in the comparison of historical traditions is to see
what is positive in them. The view that art is the imitation of nature
is changed, or broadened and lifted up in cultures outside those of
Greek descent. One comes to see in the towering structure of far
different traditions views and measurements that seem germane
to the view of truth in the comparisons. These works of art open out
views at once penetrating into the supermundane, and are cata-
strophic to ordinary experience, such as the scale of the Quetzalcoatl shrine at Teotihuacan, or the remnants at Stonehenge, or the
grand plaza, somnolent with power, at Tikal.

[2] Joseph Campbell (ed.), *Spiritual Disciplines* (New York: Pantheon Books for the
Bollingen Foundation, 1960). 1. Cammerloper, M. C., "The Position of Art in the
Psychology of our Times" (1934). Papers selected from the Eranos Year Books,
Vol. IV, pp. 424-447.

Plate IV   Santiago Tlatelolco, Distrito Federal. Façade.

Such monuments are events in the history of style in which the progression seems to move by great changes, in which the tradition seems to alter its direction, or to sometimes come to its end. Sometimes these changes can be foreseen, and met. Sometimes events, like the indrift of the Nahua groups of people, bring problems that cannot be solved. ". . . The cosmic connexions that govern the history of man as a genus are entirely inaccessible to our measures."[3] The classic Maya world, the classic Mexican world in the Teotihuacan floration come to an end, and the great arts of those periods were left behind — in the case of the arts of the Teotihuacan culture, in the barbarian exploitation of their cultural debris. In comparing the Aztec floration to these earlier ones, it seems to be made of alien matters, or tangent ones, even in law and politics. Its style is not that of inwardness and deep piety, but rather one of fear and the savagery of cult politics. This is alien and also, it happens, a late civilization mode. The Spanish conquest thus came upon societies that had to look far back in time to recall the flowering of the great culture period from which they hoped, and so vainly, to have been derived. That time had been the seventh century. The great cities of the period were now long forgotten, and some actually buried; all was confused under the barbaric Chichimec developments.

The grand phenomenon of seemingly only overt destruction involved in the Spanish conquest goes in the opposite direction here from the position often taken in history. For in a remarkably short time there was a great resurgence of creative activity that it is pos-

[3] Oswald Spengler, *The Decline of the West;* II, *Perspectives of World History* (New York: Alfred A. Knopf, Inc., 1928), p. 36.

Plate V   Santiago Tlatelolco, Distrito Federal. Side view.

sible to watch nowhere but in Mexico. It was the collapse of the
Aztec power that the Spanish secured. The Aztec supremacy obtained in religious politics, and nourished forms of depolarization.
In the Spanish conquest, after the effects of the impact were ame-
liorated in some places, a new life arose, the results of which attract us still to visit this floration, and persuade us to stay there.
"The simple empirical fact is," says George Kubler, "that the Indians were not exterminated by colonization in Mexico, and that
their labor produced an intricate, abundant and qualitative material
culture. That their absolute productive capacity increased during
the sixteenth century cannot be questioned, in spite of the loss of
numbers through epidemic disease."[4]

The meaningful work slowly grew up again under a not too dis-
similar ordering of the world. The new order was not under the
malevolence of the Amerind mythos. Work as sacrifice in cooperation with supernal forces, still, in other terms, carried on the good
of the world after the Conquest and it all came so to be understood.
The Christian calendar-round could be supported with much less
effort; indeed, that was an Indian argument against it. There was,
they owned, now too little sacred and necessary work. Before the
Conquest, work, no matter how difficult, had in a sense been enjoy-
able in its meaning. Afterwards, it tended to become toil that was
eventually involved with money. The insolence and inutility of money

[4] George Kubler, *Mexican Architecture of the Sixteenth Century* (New Haven:
Yale University Press, 1948), II, pp. 417-418. Published under the direction of the
Department of History for the Department of the History of Art in the Graduate School.

Plate VI   Santo Domingo Yanhuitlan, Oaxaca. Façade.

seemed very great to this people which had not even had the bow and arrow before the Chichimec invasion.

The strength and power of the ancient classic religion and its symbols show their effects on some later design. The myths and their symbols filtered, much altered of course, through the civilization period that followed the destruction of the classic cultures. There were changes in the modes of piety. This emerged soon in the Spanish occupation. Anyone who has ever walked into the atrium enclosure of San Francisco at Cholula recognizes the ancient scale. The scale employed here comes of no Chichimec usage either at Tenochtitlan — to trust restoration perspectives — or from Cholula. It is more likely from classic usage such as one sees at San Juan Teotihuacan. It is monumental, and it evokes awe. It has not been translated into the tiresome colossal. The colossal in current Mexican taste refers to Chichimec monuments seen at the time of the Conquest, and plentifully recalled in nostalgic modes of the twentieth century. The monumental structures pertain to classic tradition, that is, before 900 A.D.

"Tradition," says George Santayana, "in its arts is cumulative, and it interprets the whole."[5] In a world where tradition suffers no denigration the maker of things is far more important than the person we now merely call the artist. He is man, the maker, the craftsman in the real aspect of his supernatural source. He apprehends entities in his subconscious mind, and he is enabled, by right

[5] See *The Philosophy of Santayana,* edited by Irwin Edman, The Modern Library (New York: Random House, 1942), pp. 217-256.

22

Plate VI-A   Santo Domingo Yanhuitlan, Oaxaca. Façade.

training, to draw upon them. It is after the manner of the great sculptor calling forth the figure out of the marble, not beating it out, not hacking it out. Called forth thus are the forms of the Absolute as the Mahayāna has it, forms in differentiation, available to intuition, in a learning where intuition as a modality of knowledge is nurtured.

It is the assumption of the unbetrayed contact with tradition that gives the sense of power that we feel in making contact with the classic stages of the pre-Cortesian culture. The matter has been set forth in many ways and forms in the tradition of India. It is the Mahat, the Great, "a phase of consciousness beyond the ego in which there is no differentiation between the subject and the object."[6] The ego enters the situation as the agent, and is astonished at the work it has been enabled to perform. This may be any work that has to be envisaged to be made. For man, the maker, is an artist in all that he brings to completion. God, someone has said, worked and rested; man makes and adores. It may be a statue, a work of design in engineering, or an epic, or the Teotihuacan masks, or a myth stated, even to the doctrine of the samvartatthahi, in which the universes gradually move toward their Void.[7]

[6] Stella Kramrisch, *The Art of India* (London: The Phaidon Press, 1935), p. 14.

[7] Wm. E. Soothill and Lewis Hodous, *A Dictionary of Chinese Buddhist Terms* (London: Kegan Paul, Trench, Trubner & Co., Ltd., 1937). Epochs in the Mahakalpa, the Time Cycle. ". . . Samvarta Kalpa, destruction first by fire, then water, then fire, then deluge, then a great wind, in 64 stages; then Samvartatthati Kalpi, total destruction gradually reaching the Void," 85b.

Speculation on such matter is endless. In *The Future of Man* (New York: Harper and Row, Publishers, 1964) Pêre Pierre Teilhard de Chardin has said "It is difficult

Plate VI-B   Santo Domingo Yanhuitlan, Oaxaca. Side view.

The Doom occurs more frequently in the Mesoamerican scene than it does in the Buddhist retelling in the Indian account. It is the living in a more brief life-span picture that makes the work of the artist so fearfully anonymous, that gives it imminence. The maker "converts what was required by the myth into an element of formal configuration."[8] Far from having to do with mere art, it was understood that what was behind the forms, that were effective conjurations, was the protection of the operation from malice by magic. The elements of fear and goodwill that grew along with the operation of magic became the basis of religious emotion: fear, awe and love.

The nature forces under the persuasion of exercises in magic were eventually personified. Personification is the mode of abstraction available to some kinds of earlier thinking. The personification finally reveals the Gods, who are eventually observed to act in rhythmic patterns. The works of the makers were conceived within this evidence with the hope of cooperation. The powers that were

to imagine what form the ending of a world might take. A sidereal disaster would correspond nearly enough to our individual deaths. But this would entail the ending of the Earth rather than that of the Cosmos, and it is the Cosmos itself that must disappear" (p. 306, and, further, p. 307). "At this moment, St. Paul tells us (1 Cor. XV, 23 *et seq.)* when Christ shall have emptied of themselves all those powers created (rejecting that which is an element of dissociation and super-animating all that is the force of unity) He will consummate the universal unification by delivering Himself in His entire and adult body, with a capacity for union that is at length perfected to the embrace of the Diety." This is a continuous and not a cyclic form, such as obtains in Amerind and Hindu views, for here there is no *moksa.* In considering the art of Mexico one is never far from eschatological matters.

[8] Paul Westheim, *The Sculpture of Ancient Mexico,* p. 12.

Plate VI-C   Santo Domingo Yanhuitlan, Oaxaca. Interior.

honored were near, they were ready in Mexico to destroy, and to destroy fearfully. The chiliastic sense is vivid. To cease to watch, to cease to be vigilant of magical control might release the convergences in full flood, say of Papaloapan water. The more nature in its rhythms was scrutinized, the more entities there were to be personified, and the greater the weight of ritual, and of formal education for it, becomes.[9] With this, the proliferation of time-unit deities in the Maya outlook becomes understandable. It becomes easy to understand the multitude of symbols seen everywhere. Of the debris of the pre-Cortesian cultures around Mitla there were some seven thousand pieces of modelled clay sculpture mostly in abstract symbolic form in the Museo Zapoteco. Everywhere beyond these symbols the little votive figurines, most likely for propitiating vegetal growth, abound, often in the open fields.

Then there is the symbol we take so much for granted. It is the stair, the "going up." When we go up the steps of the shrine, it is not the feet that mount, but the psyche. This comes out in the preponderance of the *tepic,* the sign for the hill one mounts, appearing as a dominant symbol over Central America and Mexico. The stair is everywhere, and wherever you look there is something of a redemption symbol: the stair, the raised shrine, the towers reaching, and the fine dome. Many thousands of domes were built up to 1800. But it is under the old Maya cities in Guatemala that the stair is so patently significant. It turns up elaborately at Uaxactun

[9] George C. Vaillant, *The Aztecs of Mexico* (Baltimore: Penguin Books, Inc., 1956), Chapter X, "Religion," p. 168.

Plate VII   Santiago Cuilapan, Oaxaca. The Second Basilica.

in pyramid E-VII-sub. Nearby, at Tikal, it is likely the incipient form. Subsequently, it rises to the top of the super-imposed substructures, in five temples each nearly two hundred feet high. At Copán, the stair is splendidly integrated into the four sides of various courts. They ascend from larger courts below. At Piedras Negras, there are arrangements using courts and stairs that seem to mount in a kind of counterclockwise growth, supreme and superb.[10]

Later in the civilization period this stairway relates more and more to architectural design, rather than to iconography. It not only dominates the design of the shrine, it seems to become more and more enlarged. It is exploited with magnificence, as at the Temple of the Warriors, at Chichén-Itzá II. It is used with ineptitude added to the Wind Temple at Calixtlahuaca, and at Río Bec and at Xpuhil, both in Quintana Roo, the stair as a symbol seems at a low point of misunderstanding. It is no stair. It is like a vertical ladder panel, plastered on a shallow tower form.

The chief interest in this matter of Río Bec is the swiftness with which the significant use of symbolic form has declined, right at the end of the classic period. Indeed, working in the thick piedmont

[10] J. Eric S. Thompson, *The Rise and Fall of Maya Civilization* (Norman: University of Oklahoma Press, 1954). See Miss Tatiana Proskouriakoff's restorations following p. 66: Plate 2a, Uaxactún; 2 b, Copán; Plate 3b, Piedras Negras. Note the line of stelae. Note Plate 3a, "Palace at Sayil, Yucatán," where the stair begins to dominate, not only to emphasize, the entire acropolis. Note especially Plate 7b, Xpuhil, in Quintana Roo, where the chief culture period's symbols have been used in senility, and where the fatuously colossal, as such, first asserts itself.

Plate VII-A   Santiago Cuilapan, Oaxaca.

jungle of Uaxactún, the explorers of those vital sites did not even know of Río Bec, found much later, though only a few miles away.

Here this decline manifests itself on a building, the pyramid character of which has withered away. The building stands on a platform that is hardly even a low substructure. It has two towers, each topped with a crest. All the symbolic elements are misapplied, and the usual statement carried by ornament has become empty. The symbols are decorations, and the plateau of complete decay is achieved.

This situation is the completed form of a cultural demise. When the symbol is gone, the doctrine is gone. Whatever is decorative only, and no longer belongs to the vernacular of ornament, is ossification. It does not necessarily recall its origin or any significance. Thus, in the Hodegitria, the awesome revelation of supernatural majesty in Byzantine Christianity becomes after the renaissance the Mother and Child that does not any longer connote the Incarnation, but merely a humanistic convention. And here, too, the Sacred Stair has become only a vertical ladder panel. Thus, Río Bec[11] reveals that theocratic tradition in architecture has come to the inept. Its style has changed. The Chenes, the Puuc, the Toltecs, Chichén-Itzá II, and the Mayapán times all lie in the future. And in the end, the invaders were all modified to conformation under what was left of Maya civilization, itself much changed.

[11] Pál Kelemen, *Medieval American Art* (New York: The Macmillan Company, 1956), Plate 28, a and b.

Plate VII-B   Santiago Cuilapan, Oaxaca.

In the culture period there is a common iconography and a consistent growth in style in the terms of it. In the civilization period that follows there is an iconography depolarized by new elements. It seemed, up to a very short time ago, that there was no Feathered Serpent symbol to be seen at Tikal. But in the Second Empire, as the palladium of the Toltecs, it is seen in the north of Yucatán everywhere.

The stair then for the Old Empire was something very near a prime symbol. The evidence of its fading away here suggests other forms that we do not know disappearing in the same way. Or it suggests earlier usages of things that have survived in curtailed meaning and form — the languages, the liturgies employed on the rich sites, the theologies involved, and the forms and uses of music. There would have to be a vitiation of these forms after 708 A.D. in the Old Empire, for of course the very purpose of such revolutions is to shed the metaphysical wealth that the new people in control cannot manipulate and, of course, cannot understand. It wasn't the Uto-Aztecs who would have been innately hospitable to these things as categories, nor was it the Toltecs, nor the Nahuas, nor the people who "guarded" Huitzilopochtli in a sacramental meal. After all the ruin of culture system by barbarians, and the wreckage of barbarian civilizations in the Conquest, it was the Franciscans who could be hospitable to the deeper recollections that might come out in new forms if life became stabilized again.

The Tlaloc mask, the common element in design in the Old Empire is common, and prominent, but its significance is clearly fading, and it has become weakened by repetition as an all-over pattern in

28

Plate VIII   San Francisco, Tepeaca, Puebla. Vaulting.

the Puuc style, as at Kabah. One might say it still has authenticity but much lessened power. (Plate XLV.) It is now architecture, rather than doctrine, and so its power is vitiated.

There was here, by this time, something like the Hellenistic period that was anything but Greek, and was, here, anything but Maya — somnolent cities sleeping their days away when the center of power has passed to other places. There, Athens and Alexandria, Axun and Edessa were watching the strength of Rome uncoil. And in northern Yucatán, Kabah and Labna, the later Chichén and Dzibilchaltún gave in to the inexorable histories of the Nahua. While power creeps away, sophistication grows as buildings increase in size and fragility of finished ornament. As the delicate masks of Kabah are weakened on the wall with each succeeding rain, one remembers the primeval power that even in photographs informs the gigantic balustrade masks that border the stair in E-VII-sub Uaxactún. They were living terror.

This has no aftermath, for in the Maya country, mostly the cultural soil is shallow. But the religious authenticity of the classic Teotihuacan, dormant in the Nahua centuries, rises again in the alien style forms of color that is now vitreous. The low gamut of Teotihuacan lyric fresco is then seen no more, but color asserts itself in hues available in Talavera glazes, in high values and high intensities.

It is this color that one sees in almost any direction, going to Puebla and Cholula and south to Acatlan. It is not quite the gold of Meshed, or the greyed-blue of the Mosque of Isphanan, but candid yellow and the lower blue of Andalusia.

Plate IX   Ixmiquilpan, Hidalgo. Vault of transept crossing.

For color, it has seemed, is, besides authentic subtle use of scale, another intimation of latent power. Fragments of fresco and evidences of formalized design as well as narrative passages show what the sovereign classic outlook could do with color. For the periods of alien barbarian art there is a wider use of color surviving. Among the barbarians the use of symbolic color sometimes suggests Mongolian recollections and, in another connection, the seeming prevalence of color in high value suggests Ch'ing propensities, especially in the theatre, among the lower tone values of Ming. This is the wide range of color and sheen effects in the use of feathers, for the panaches of various ranks, for liturgical costume of all kinds, and for other things, such as a kind of inlay. The richer Iberian technique released much wider use of color in Mexican art, and the floration of vitreous sheens and scales of glaze values is so outstanding that it gives reason to pause over it. Certainly they took to the new color everywhere, and the ease of procuring glaze effects without laboriously rubbing one hard stone on another, and getting moreover glaze effects in color, was lost on no one. Glitter, the concealment by light of form and color in late arts, came to characterize whole cities in the seventeenth century, and some of it can still be seen in the general urban aspect as one goes across the Valley of Puebla.

And far more to the point, in this same valley one comes across glimpses of a veritable inwardness of uses of color — color for its own sake — in some of the exploration of glaze tile resources. If the arresting gate to the atrium of San Francisco Acatepec in carved

30

Plate X   A church near San Cristóbal de las Casas, Chiapas.

brick shows a flair for the new materials, what is shown by the façade of the basilica in unglazed low orange, glazed cold yellow, blue and white. The gateway is a complete mastery of the material carried off in the manner of a spirited cadenza. The façade is no chromatic novelty of a happy peasantry, such as the church about two blocks south is, but a striking master's achievement that, once seen, never fades away in the recollection, but grows in it.

But these are nothing beside what yet may be seen at the same place. The little bell towers are also of carved brick and concrete plaster, and extended with twisted Solomonic colonettes, covered with plaster that holds fragments of tile. This is all a very old usage, of course, and with jewels you see it on Orcagna's altar setting in the Or San Michele and, now that one thinks of it, in many other places. In the bright daylight all this augmented glaze color winks and speculates in the light, and the forced gaze pushes far. Fragmented emeralds and crushed opals make but a pathetic analogy to what then happens when you see these towers after a rain. "Everyone knows we have the finest church in the world," said a Mexican farm girl of this place. She knows best its gold interior, and she thus disposes of some three hundred other churches within a radius of five miles.

Thus the best in art is good works. The intention of good works is the drawing of merit for salvation. Once more, anticipating the later consideration of these matters under viceregal art, we see how little the Erasmian program would have helped the Mexican Ecclesia. In good works for salvation the Latin Church knows what it

31

Plate XI   San Pablo Yuriria, Querétaro. Façade.

does. It works well. Holiness abounds in the cohesion of the parish, shown in a thousand places in such contributions and such dedicated labor. Faith, without the perfection of art in good works, is dead.

This varied, profound employment of color seems to me to be the evidence of great inwardness. The quality of inwardness seemed apparent in classic architecture and sculpture. In sculpture this quality appears best in the masks. The few that survive are represented wonderfully by the mask in dark slate from Cholula, in a private collection in Mexico City.[12] Though small, only a few inches in height, this mask is a work of simplicity, power and inwardness without equal in New World art. It is the completed organization of abstraction in symbolic form that appears in the reality of the classic style. With immense and pregnant subtlety the planes are left very broad; there is no approach to natural form anywhere, yet in the filing of the open lips and the lowered eyelids there is human feeling with unalloyed understanding. But it is not pathos in Praxiteles' sense. All the provincial naturalism of the preclassic floration is left behind. It is a radiantly ideoplastic work, in which technique revels in itself and its paradoxical ability to surrender content above all manner.

On the same order, but removed rather than brought to human

[12] Imgard Groth-Kimball, *The Art of Ancient Mexico* (London: Thames & Hudson, 1954), Plate 25.

Plate XII   San Pablo Yuriria, Querétaro. Tower.

feeling is the monolithic Goddess of the Waters, Chalchiuhtlicue at Teotihuacan, a terror symbol organized in straight and heavy lines and iron shadows brutally confining spaces containing relevant symbols in small borders, all under complete magical evocation and certain claustrophobic confinement.

In a far later time the *contrast* of this work with the Aztec Mother Goddess Coatlicue, another monolith, shows not the exaltedly remote aesthetics of the classic outlook, but the near. Here in the Coatlicue there is the architect and the sculptor rather than the assemblage of hierophant's fear forms in less effective, physio-plastic aspect. There is the anthropomorphized formality of skulls and serpent heads in double confrontation for hypnotic paralysis, and effective it most certainly is, in most immanent presence, all on heavy columnar legs and feet — a projection of raw force that could not move. This is a telling confrontation of Aztec immaturity beside the classic power of the Water Goddess of olden times.

Across the mountains, at Tenochtitlan, other aspects of eastern parallels occur. There is the ancient chieftainship, the priest-king, that in so many modes has been with us. There is the protocaliphate of Diocletian and Constantine holding the world together as pontiff and princeps and the culmination in the overwhelming grandeur for Justinian of the Agia Sophia, a mosque-form, the world-cavern for the ruler who can persuade doctrine into dogma and rule with it. Here, in Mexico, this great convergence has reached a somewhat similar suggestive grandeur in scale. The ruler can see no end to the expansion of the state, at least to the south. He, too, comes to

Plate XIII   San Pablo Yuriria, Querétaro. Front view.

his place as pontiff, and his data, as well as his intentions, come from star lore, with a foreign policy based, let us say, on astrology, an extension for him of an ecclesiastical education and a life of dynastic politics.

It is through the congealing of this cultural lava over the Nahua landscape that the ancient classic soul had to break, after centuries of repression by the northerners. In the siege of Mexico, Cortés actually strove to restrain the fury of the Nahua allies against the Tenochca state. It was to their interest to kill; it was to his interest to conserve. This he accomplished only toward the end of the siege, with a restraining hand. The Nahua allies had fought desperately. For Indians are truly men, as the carpetbaggers later had to be reminded again in the *Sublimis Deus* of Paul III. For when the savage invasions hit the old classic cultures of Mexico, they did not have much to go on themselves to develop after the impact. There was destruction, possession and great cultural envy even to genealogical adaptation. Even in the myths of Chichimec barbarism the envy to reconstruct some destroyed views can be seen. The modes were now pursued with political violence, in the strife of war. Moreover, it would often seem that human sacrifice in the classic periods was liturgical only. But the direction taken by the trait of sacrifice in the civilization period cults seems not to have belonged to the older cults. Quetzalcoatl is a brother to Osiris and Heracles, types of the Savior. But is Tonatiuh to be seen as a Savior, albeit in a sort of reverse term? Likely not. The blood demand is one thing, but, in addition, the picture of sacrifice given by Bernal Díaz del

Plate XIV　　　　San Pablo Yuriria, Querétaro. Façade, plateresque detail.

Castillo is that it had a casual, widespread, cannibalistic, secular aspect as well as a liturgical one.

In some of the needs that were current, the practice of the sacrifice was a necessity. But at the best and highest of the connotations, it was a great burden. We cannot bear the remembrance of the Creatures of the Immolation, and one cannot forget them. There was an earlier consecration in the blood that flowed down the *teocalli* stair. In one southern Mexican codex the account is given of the sacrifice of a prominent man in a sacred war (a Mixteca episode, described by Spinden); the same account shows him assisting, earlier, at the sacrifice of one of his brothers. Later the cries were lost in the low conch blare, and in the low and sluggish throb of the serpent-skin drums, but the echoes have never died away. The inwardness that would have made the Quetzalcoatl legend the myth to carry effective redemption power, intimated in the Morning Star resurrection, faded away before the cruder forces. For redemption was far from the work of the later Chichimecs, and Quetzalcoatl remains the great figure of the dying sun.[13] There is small place for redemption in the Tlaloc-Tezcatlipoca fusion that obtained at Tenayuca, and less place for it in the fusion of Tlaloc-Huitzilopochtli at Tenochtitlan. For here the affairs of throne and

[13] Ignacio Bernal, *Mexico Before Cortez* (New York: Doubleday & Company, Inc., 1963), p. 83. See also Herbert S. Spinden, "Indian Manuscripts of Southern Mexico," *Smithsonian Report for 1933,* pp. 429-451.

altar were deeply intermixed.[14] Into this last phase of the appalling will-to-power walked Hernando Cortés, his soldiers, his Mercedarian and his secular cleric.[15] These two, and some later clerics, were the forerunners of the exalted Twelve Apostles of the great Cardinal Cisneros' Franciscan venture. Under them, architecture and most of the auxiliary arts became a Mexican program. A setting thus is to be made for the long latent resources of style, where classic inwardness opens up again in the resources of viceregal splendor.

[14] Dexter Allen, *The Coil of the Serpent* (New York: Coward-McCann, Inc., 1956). An admirable historical novel of the last days of the Texcocan State. In its sequel, *The Valley of Eagles,* the debacle is brought up to the eve of the Conquest.

[15] Bernal Díaz del Castillo, *The True History of the Conquest of New Spain,* many editions. See especially *The Bernal Díaz Chronicles: The True Story of the Conquest of Mexico,* edited by Albert Idell (New York: Doubleday & Co., 1956), Chapter XVI. In the matter of translations the Idell work is outstanding not only for simple candor, but for simple honesty.

IN THE STUDY of cultures it is the role of style that has supreme value. With style the forms begin the growth that is to make up the matrix of the culture. Style is the essential accomplishment of the culture, and the sum of its actuality. Before it begins there is something of a unity in the groups, the tribes, the clans and the clan divisions. And when the culture that will drive toward completion has emerged, there is then something like one vista for all the group. It not only remains one. Each person, each movement, each pattern, each accomplishment, each "family," home, form, name, shrine made, burial form is drawn deeper and deeper into the social amalgam. To be outside of it is eventually scarcely comprehensible no matter how great the culture burden. There would be no place to go except backward; there would be nothing to do, except to do nothing.

As one form is set, accompanying forms are given direction. The mode that these forms take together comes to be thought of as style. When the culture thus begins, its history begins; when the forms of the culture have been completed in their potential, the culture comes to an end. Thenceforth, choice is eclectic. In culture there is amalgam; in civilization there is mixture. The mixture can be one of unrelated forms and matter. The whole is no longer capable of directional form, except where its specializations become rigid, enlarged, and finally ungovernable.

In almost any cultural situation the beginning that can be described is certainly not early. Egypt was old indeed when the Horus cult, coming from the East, set, in burial custom and in architecture, the forms that were to characterize the art of the Old Empire. In the Americas, and especially in the Maya world, the growth that was clothed with the style started in the form of the shrine.

The revealed pyramid E-VII-sub at Uaxactún in the Petén in Guatemala is dated as a late formative period monument.[16]

The pyramid is twenty-seven feet high. On the top of it, set back from the edges, is the substructure of the small temple *cella* that once stood there. There are four substructures, as such, for the pyramid itself beneath this top one, each enlarging in area and volume as it approaches the ground. Up the middle of each side of the whole structure rises a stairway that on each side is bordered, or rather, as one should say in such a connection, guarded, by masks. On the outside of the mask balustrade is a small stair for a part of the entire height.

The masks are theriomorphs, composite animal forms that converge supernatural power symbols into the winged lion, for example, or the gigantic winged bull gods and kings at Khorsabad, or like Ezekiel's seraphim whose thrice-repeated paired wings, "with touch of fire," visually secure the Ineffable.

At Tikal, which is very near Uaxactún, the masks of E-VII-sub appear again at Temple II. But here they are high in the air on the

[16] J. Eric S. Thompson, *The Rise and Fall of Maya Civilization,* Plate 5c (following p. 66), E-VII sub, Uaxactún, Petén. Formative Period, ca. 325.

Plate XV   San Pablo Yuriria, Querétaro. Façade detail.

great vertical comb above the *cella*. The mask does not appear com-
monly in late sites, like Copán, in this giant form. But this feline
mask, derived not ultimately from the jaguar as a power symbol,
survives throughout the whole Amerind history in small forms, to
the end; extending thus throughout the whole growth, having had
its origin, it seems, in the *tao-ti'eh* mask of eastern areas of the
Pacific Basin cultures. Indeed, every once in a while it awakens
vivid recollections of Late Chou.

With it, at Tikal, in the still uncleared jungle around Temple V,
at least one building, a small rectangular one, has on the corner
of the upper panel of the façade the Tlaloc mask with the long
curved nose, and this is a symbol that comes out most prominently
indeed in façade designs in the purer style buildings of the New
Empire, in northern Yucatán. At Kabah the mask touches the ground
and rises as a repeat pattern over the whole façade, clear to the
crest, restated over the structure, as may be seen in marvelously
broad convention in Plate XLV and Plate XLVI.

And it is here at this next site of the Maya culture that there is
to be seen the characteristic form of the pyramid for classic Maya
times. The pyramid now approaches nearly two hundred feet in
height. The substructures have become very high, and there are
several of them. The temple is set back on top of the highest substructure, and there is in front of it only a ledge — a narrow ledge,
hardly a yard wide. This platform is reached by a stairway, imposed
at an alien plane on the whole pyramid. At Tikal there are five of
these great structures, four arranged in ceremonial relation to each
other, and groups of temples and smaller buildings, some joined

Plate XVI   San Agustín Acolman, Mexico, Distrito Federal.
Façade detail.

to others by very wide causeways bordered by parapets. At Copán
and some other cities the forms are similarly monumental, but not
on the monumental vertical as at Tikal. As time goes on, the pyramid
seems to sink back into the mass of related structures, somewhat
as it seems to have done after Fourth Dynasty times in Egypt. From
these structures the cultures to the north in Yucatán seem to have
derived, in part, somewhat similar forms. Much farther to the north,
in the Valley of Mexico, and at a much earlier date, the elevated
dance worship floor and altar had been raised at Cuicuilco that
Byron Cummings and others dated, at first, to a most venerable
antiquity.

For quite a long time the pyramid remains the dominant form for
the Maya centers. But, as at Piedras Negras and other later classic
Maya sites, there is a drawing together of the bases of the substructures to make an enclosed court or dance area, from each
side of which steps to the pyramid's steps rise. The whole complex
seems to draw together in these units, as they are at the same time
proliferated. They seem, as at Copán and Piedras Negras, somewhat
to move counterclockwise, and this could be said of the group of
tightly related courts on the north acropolis at Monte Albán, too.
But in each case it may be found that there were topographical
limitations.

Eventually the pyramid, the elaborate succession of substructures, fades away, until there is only the basic platform as the chief
consideration. But the pyramid, and all that goes with it on the
ornamental, that is the significant side of society, has gone. The
mere craft tradition of applied ornament, not a related matter, goes

Plate XVII   La Santısima, Mexico, Distrito Federal. Façade,
upper storeys.

on, speaking no longer the metaphysical language of the older ornament, but becoming a tradition of applied decoration. What had been stated, in stucco, on E-VII-sub goes on to at least the cresting of the façade of Temple II, on the Grand Plaza at Tikal, but it hardly moves farther in the same mode. Other phases of the tradition turn up, serene with power, at Copán, and at Palenque it states, in high-minded subtlety, some of the best relief sculpture ever made.

Of several examples, this pyramid may suffice to illustrate the time and development involved in the culture form. As in religion, when the symbol is gone the doctrine fades; here, when the potential of the culture symbol seems exhausted, it has no power left. By the time the pyramid and its relevant sculture record is worked out at Tikal, the life of the site is over. This comes soon to be true not only of ancillary sites down the Usumacinta River, but its truth applies even more swiftly to sites up the river. The symbols lose their power, and come to be without significance. Even at Río Bec, a short distance from Uaxactún and Tikal, the platform is not in the old Maya sense formally a substructure. Even more astonishingly it is not even a *tepic*.

By the time this account of a phase of style was over within Guatemala, it had gone through something of the same history in the Valley of Mexico. Teotihuacan had fallen, and its folk had moved, many going to Azcapotzalco. The Toltec gifts of aggressive organization point toward the future, toward the Aztec beginnings. The traits, the symbols that the Toltecs absorbed and borrowed from the classic cultures are all transformed for the use of the new and alien emphasis in the new eclectic times under the barbarians. For

Plate XVIII   Santa Prisca, Taxco, Guerrero. Façade, upper storeys.

from thence on, to the coming of the men of Cortés, it is the barbarian worldview that obtains. Barbarians could no more have understood the nameless subtle splendor of Teotihuacan in its serene reaches than Mahmud of Ghazni could have apprehended the richness of the Gujarat culture at the Somanātha-Pātan. The proof, as usual, lies in the later attempt to cherish the classic tradition, and to exalt it, after its back has been broken; then to make full use of it.

Indeed, so effective was the transition from the classic culture to that of the Toltecs, that the Toltecs and others came to refer to Teothihuacan as the home of the Gods, and later Chichimecs referred to the Toltecs themselves as masters of crafts and architecture. With these traditions there was also passed along the tradition of a script. The script had been developing after the astrological data was recorded. In stellar observations for astrological purposes, these cultures would have made a contribution to general knowledge. But a demotic script to carry it lay far in the future, in the proliferation of the painted manuscripts. [17]

In these notable works very great accomplishment lay in design. One of the delights of the study of neolithic cultures is the clear relationship that appears between materials, forms and techniques. Writing, viewed as painting, was a very advanced art. Among its prominent uses was that of record-keeping of all kinds, in which the data are ideographs and pictographs in color on paper or vellum, and painted with pens or brushes of various width on the glazed

[17] Sir Alan Gardiner, *Egyptian Grammar* (London: Oxford University Press, 1950), pp. 5, 10. This suggests the time involved in the development of literary demotic.

Plate XIX   La Valenciana, Guanajuato, Guanajuato. Sacristy door.

surface in symbolic color — white and black, rose, orange, silver, purple, green, red, yellow, blue, ochre, sepia, grey; probably in all cases there was the beginning at least of phonetic indication in the glyphs, among their various functions. It starts out like the Egyptian history of script, but it did not get as far along in the development. Chinese ideographs are phonetic, their pictographic residue is of interest to the archaic story of semantics. Likely in Mexico a manuscript could be read in parts through more than one discipline. But the writing-painting style was consistent, and it all moved along, it seems, to a script that was sometimes as advanced as what we would call stenographic, and in a manner, here and there, of what we would call cursive. Probably the most attractive is the Maya work, the Dresden Codex.

The motivation is first that of record-keeping, eventually for taxation data. But the recording of data for astrological reflection and usage carries the development into history, literature, and especially into the whole field of liturgical controls. The essential story of this growth is over with by the end of the classic period. Postclassic cultures, with alien rhythms and generalized intention, made another art of the script tradition.

The need to read astrological data from the accumulation of long observation led to the interest in what we would call history. The history in Maya times has a limited style that changes radically when one looks at mixture documents where running variation is employed in grouped pictographs, in rhythms unknown in the classic period. History is concerned with what is worthwhile to record: the proceeding of the God-world, and its incidence to mundane affairs.

43

Plate XX   Natividad de Nuestra Señora, Tepoztlan, Morelos. Façade, main doorway.

In these respects it is needful to refresh our sympathy in judging what history is and what it does. It is a mode of reflection not bound to literary skill or allegiances, or overtones. A first fact in this interest is the nature of the limitations involved. These limitations come from within the reflective life. They are involved with views that are to be held. We do not object to the history of our own country being written from the point of view of economics and sociology. When we use the same view for other countries, the history does not seem to be whole. One could say that it is not banking that makes Mexico to be clear in the view, but, let us say, grace.

So, in the matter of what is called science. Science is the way employed, in each culture, to describe its physical world-around. Since we do not use the measures of astrology, in our view we make short work of cultures that have employed this outlook. This, in judging cultures from their own point of view, is our distortion. In the United States, scholarship is only comfortable with the problem of using its own biases. It is in complete derogation that the term astrology is employed. Astronomy, a unique development in the West, is a term that is substituted. But astronomy is employed in the exploration of space, and the element of time comes in as a part of the data of the description of it. From our point of view time is a derivation of space. In such usage the concern is with extension. But to the ancient American cultures time is likely rather to appear to be just an entity. It is not concerned with stellar space as such, but with human fate. The end was not celestial mathematics, but consolation.

The Maya usage, when a strong clear causality was invoked,

Plate XXI   San Miguel, *Posa del Atrio,* Huejotzingo, Puebla.

in its earlier period, had this matter as its metaphysical drive. We can see after Toltec times, and perhaps in those times, how this drive was reduced to fear alone, assuaged eventually by blood of all kinds, of all kinds available qualitatively, as well as in quantity, great quantity, as the starving sun could faint, as it were, on the morning horizon. But in Maya times the task was to keep track of divine entities, their force, attributes and actions. The folk existed through helping the Gods in this gigantic task of sustaining the cosmic order.[18] The elements observed were personified. That was their mode of reality, and secondarily of scientific description. Thus the personifications were naturally deified. This is hardly the matter of astronomy. It reveals an historic sense of profound care; it presupposes a long record, and, equally important, a script.

The script galvanizes the increased unity that has become the core of the culture.[19] This the Mesoamericans were achieving, as had the Nile folk, the people of Sumer, and the scholars of the dynasty of Shang and Chou. In their times, before the convergences of forces and elements that made up the scripts, each had worked

[18] Paul Westheim, *The Sculpture of Ancient Mexico,* p. 2.

[19] Oswald Spengler, *The Decline of the West; II, Perspectives of World History,* p. 36. "But the history of script belongs integrally with the expression-history of the several higher cultures. That the Egyptian, Chinese, Babylonian, and Mexican each formed a special script in its pre-Cultural age — that the Indian and the Classical on the other hand did not do so, but took over (and very late) the highly developed writing of a neighboring Civilization — that in the Arabian, again, every new religion and sect immediately formed its particular script — all these are facts that stand in a deeply intimate relation to the generic form — history of these cultures and its inner significance."

Plate XXII   San Miguel, Huejotzingo, Puebla. Tequitqui Cross.

out a complete expression for itself that, along with the magical and liturgical activities thus recorded, was the basis of the more unified culture of later neolithic times. These developments, converging in writing and drawing forms that were of course at first identical, appear first in the wonderful seeming maturity of the Leyden Plaque. It bears the date of 320 A.D.

It is, in the matter of its way of incised drawing, a complex affair of art styles and date inscriptions that is anything but rudimentary. The Leyden Plaque was set in what became the crowded rhythms and calligraphy of the stelae and the codices. This attitude survived in the Chichimec writing — an alien spirituality using an earlier authentic form — and it comes out, of course, in the post-Cortesian times in various ways. There, in the prevalence of what may be called static movement, the baroque equipoise, the only direction remaining is that of plasticity, burgeoning in the third dimension.

Quite close in date to the Leyden Plaque, bearing a now definitely calligraphic script, is a famous mortuary bowl. The dish is in the National Museum in Guatemala City. It is a discovery of the Carnegie Institute working at Uaxactún in 1931. In the script drawing of the one dancing figure, the attitude toward line is that of late, very late work. This is the episode on the interior of a cascabel plate in pinkish orange, painted in black. Part of the interest here is in the script around the edge of the plate. The statement so written is said to have *only* a decorative (so early!) significance. But that is the cavalier attitude toward writing complicated dates with a brush in running script, as shown in a cylindrical vase discovered in the same secondary vault. Here the statement is a formal date.

Plate XXII-A   San Miguel, Huejotzingo, Puebla. High altar.

These examples are the reverse side of the infinite care and
assurance of the script carved in the planks of the wooden ceiling
at Tikal, Temple IV, and in the discoveries at Tikal in white marble
with glyphs carved with the care used for jade, and, one should
suggest, done with the point of view used for jade, the groove edge
first squared, and then rounded. The breathless care, the clarity,
the richly involved detail, the prevalence and extent of the style
show the substances of deep piety and late artistic scholarship
conjoined in action. They are in the grand style. But apparently
available long before this time was the writing with the brush,
likely to be a kind of proto-demotic, rolling, calligraphic and stenographic script at the same time.

Events in style as it is later to appear seem to bring forth recollections of some of these works on late formative and early classic
art. In contemplating the opulent convolutions of design in some
Mexican seventeenth and eighteenth century churches in the Bajío,
in Quarétaro and in some small towns here like Salamanca, old
images emerge, and it seems then not too far to the dark symmetrical writhing, the tangle of fear-forms and their more fearful
shadows, in the Temple of the Sculptured Doorway, and from the
symmetrical gorgon-stare of the Tlaloc masks at Tikal, to the hyp-
nosis evoked by the shadow forms in the gilded wood sculpture
of the churrigueresque. Here, too, the changing light brings forth the
form, or lets it recede, as the patterns of moving shadows over the
involutions confess the flight of hours.

TO GO by the scheme that has been suggested for making the civilization period follow that of the development of the culture leaves one for most localities far adrift in Mexican art at the end of the fifteenth century. The older important Maya cities had been in ruins for half a thousand years when Moctezuma II's great fear was realized. The Zapotecs were long submerged; the Chichimec contributions absorbed. Cholula was by then under a Chichimec overlay. The post-Toltec cities around the lake were far on the decline. Texcoco was suffocated by cabals behind altars, and the Aztecs were shamelessly putting pieces of cults and other cultural debris together to make themselves respectable. Teotihuacan itself was a buried site for nomads of near-paleolithic Mazapan ways. But Tenochtitlan was in full bloom, to the state already, as someone has said, of bread and circuses. It maintained a great city-world, with other important centers, like Tlatelolco, nearby.

For its time, the fifteenth century, it was the *ville lumière.* The key to the world-city is the debris of folk, cults, arts, cultures that are gathered and that converge to such spots, to expend, or to slip into the stage of fellahin. From the far South cotton comes, and from the road from Texas Huastecan cults, and ficus paper tribute is levied wherever it can be obtained.

3

The later religiousness is likely the main clue to the problem of what the conquistadors saw in their taking over the scene in New Spain. The period when art had been the statement of power in the New World culture, in the terms of later religiousness, had been over for a long time, except for the Aztecs. In former times it was a matter of power in possession of the processes of culture; now it is a matter of having these things as spoil. Teotihuacan and Tula have been gone for centuries. Texcoco is absorbed, Cholula an appanage. The castle, in the dynastic palace in Tenochtitlan, is at the foot of the fane, the Great Temple, almost adjacent to it. The mind that states foreign policy is that of a man who is also something very close to pontiff. His education for both state and church is based on astrology, and in this world, astrology is high science. The fate of gods and men all depend upon it. It has nothing even remotely to do with what shallow history calls here astronomy. For it is not primarily stellar orbits and patterns that are watched, but here implacable divinities, concerned with fate.

In terms of the Second Maya Empire we are in the days after the destruction of Mayapán. In terms of Roman history, long after Augustus, with great "classical" cities to the quiet that comes when power goes, still sending out products of earlier exported culture yet in demand in far-off Gandhara, and in turn, unravelling late Han silks at Antioch for reweaving silk thread for gauzes in Alexandria.

There had been a complete termination of cultural dynamics save for the Aztec syncretic history. Peoples to the north, east and west had resisted most military contact successfully, but the Huastec cloisonné vase in the Anthropological Museum at Tulane is probably an important monument and it is not provincial but strikingly

Plate XXIII   Tequitqui Cross at the *Parroquia* at the Basilica of Guadalupe, Distrito Federal.

sophisticated.[20] Von Hagen makes an account of the Aztec State living on peripheral consumption goods, manufactures and pack-train carriers.[21] There were onerous compulsive operations for thirty-eight nations with Aztec garrisons. Their goods were carried in pack-trains of their own folk, used, in some cases, for sacrifice.[22]

Although there may seem to be something of a pantheistic charity in the Aztec policy, it was a forbearance that is possible to the victor. Conquest was envisaged as remaking. For those who are conquered, the creative impulse must look to other times and other places for opportunities to break through the overlying crust that the conquest, harsh and uncompromising, has made. Then, if sometimes favorable situations will allow the old visions to come through in the new forms that have been superimposed, the old may, in a seemingly altered way, flourish. Who has not stood before the

[20] Pál Kelemen, *Medieval American Art*, p. 167 and Plate 116d. Baked brown clay. In laid areas, orange, brown and cream, alternated in the same design elements, to strengthen the design in variety. Note the same device in Peruvian weaving. Plate 176a, Coast Tiahuanaco. This is a widespread device in art, but it is especially prominent in the overall canon of achievements in the art of the New World.

[21] Victor W. Von Hagen, *The Aztecs* (Cleveland: The World Publishing Company, 1958), p. 71. "... And on the tribute lists were 371 villages and tribes who had to yield the things of their land to Mexico."

[22] George Kubler, *The Art and Architecture of Ancient America* (Baltimore: Penguin Books, Inc., 1962), p. 51. "... Thereafter the Aztec Kings, as dominant partners in a triple alliance with Texcoco and Tacuba, extended their conquests to the east coast, to southern Mexico and into Central America, until the network of subject tribes included thirty-eight provinces held by Aztec garrisons and paying tribute to the cities of the Valley of Mexico."

Plate XXIV   Santiago, Tlatelolco, Distrito Federal. Entrance to school.

static convulsions of sculpture in the Convent Church of Santa Rosa in Querétaro, wood-covered with gesso bearing gold leaf, and had come out of his recollection, if only from books, the figures around the den at the top of the hieroglyph door at Copán? It is something of this sculpture that will appear one day, the art along with the architecture and the painted codices, that will survive the Aztec suffocation. From the very beginning was there not to be an "esoteric baroque" in Maya art, "a wandering and exuberant formal fantasy, that never stops inventing arabesques and paraphrases"?[23] These are the very things that appear finally out of what might at first be the infusion of architectural rigidity in the churrigueresque. For, like many passages in Maya art of far away long ago, it is filled with fresh statements and with its intrinsic comments upon them. This Maya is an art hardly like the serene and severe aspect of Teotihuacan, as shown in the exalted austerity of the stone masks and in the widespread architectural forms. And nowhere, not even in the massed platforms and superstructures of Copán, is there the grandeur of Monte Albán.

Impulses in creative work are transmitted, thus, through cultural fabrics. This is an axiom in religion, that, once stated, a doctrine and a practice are seldom dropped. In the subjective counterpart of the tradition in art, the energy of style also may emerge again as a potential, much changed, no doubt, and hardly at first to be recognized. Often in this case it becomes merely a fashion, without inwardness, but nostalgically opulent. In the tradition of style cul-

[23] Paul Westheim, *The Sculpture of Ancient Mexico*, p. 22.

Plate XXV   San Nicolás Actopan, Hidalgo. Refectory vaulting.

tural modalities can be followed. These tendencies grow along beside each other. Each has its own pattern of growth, and its own influence; each has its own ramification, until it is lost. Expanding shadows merge and evoke new connotations as at other times they lose strength in the opposite direction, grow pallid in form and content, and disappear in aridity.

In judging what the Spaniards really encountered in coming into Tenochtitlan, it is useful to see what was synthetic and what was syncretic. What was synthetic would encompass the older cults that had a long history and that had become more or less shifting entities. In a brief sketch of the Aztec calendar-round, Vaillant lists sixty-three divinities, some who preside in the calendar-round of the solar year of eighteen months and the final five days.[24] These cults would include in some cases a conjunction of mature cults that had come up through a long historical development and had been joined together, in one way or another, on the basis of some kind of similarity. Syntheses and syncretism likely are involved in the many versions of the Quetzalcoatl tradition, in which the Sejourné attempt to make an authentic redemption cult out of the Hero may, in the future investigations, have much substance.[25] Synthetic

[24] George C. Vaillant, *The Aztecs of Mexico,* p. 168. "There was little thought of the perfection of the individual when vast powers hovered close, ready to destroy the whole tribe if it ceased its vigilant watch on native." The more they scrutinized nature in its rhythms, the more entities there were to be personified, for that is the modality, and the greater the weight of ritual became.

[25] Laurette Séjourné, *Burning Water,* translated by Irene Nicholson (London, New York: Thames & Hudson, 1957).

Plate XXVI   San Agustín Acolman, Hidalgo. Fresco, black and white.

would be the long development; syncretic would be the fusion of Tenayuca and Tenochtitlan.

Both of these elements seem present at Tula, in the North Pyramid, called Lord of the House of Dawn (Tlahuizcalpantecuhtli). The Feathered Serpent, once more, represents the older cults of rain and fertility. This, here, is joined to the mystic cult of the planet Venus (another aspect, elsewhere, of the Feathered Serpent) represented by Mixcoatl, a hunting divinity whose cult required human sacrifice.[26] This is a Toltec aspect that grows in prestige, and joins eventually with another cult to dwell in the Great Temple at Tenochtitlan. In one of the morning sacrifices at this temple four hundred quail were immolated, quail with white spots on dark slate head and neck. These white spots were the stars dispersed thus by the involutions of magic, so that their brother star the sun, with now many other additional names, could arise. This was a minor part of the ritual obligation but in it we recognize the four hundred brothers of the Hero, Mixcoatl, relating, likely, to the black Tezcatlipoca of the North, of Toltec antecedents. For the great eclectic temple and its liturgies it is what one would expect: an immature culture using all the inherited credentials it can lay hands on to persuade the God to give more rain to feed a now rapidly growing megalopolis. This tendency is the pushing of the special trait of this civilization, progression by ritual. From the top of the *teocalli* from which Cortés looked down with the proud but frightened pontiff,

[26] George Kubler, *The Art and Architecture of Ancient America*, p. 47.

Plate XXVII   View of Oaxaca de Juárez (Antequera), Oaxaca, from Monte Albán.

there could scarcely be too much blood for the prana for Tonatiuh, shining above. For grave matters are at stake.

Going along the great causeway, Bernal Díaz makes the entry into Mexico a matter of very exciting times. They *were* exciting, and one comes to wonder, in the blazing of it, just what it was that appeared so gleaming to him beyond the Iberian towns he had known. The town could not have been baroque, since this phase of art had been cut off long ago, likely at the first burning of Teotihuacan. It was surely what we would call eclectic in its style, a time when the historically available style had long lost power, and had ceased to operate. The city itself was not ancient in the sense that Cholula is now, and was then. The palaces and temples were newly designed and built, and as a city of canals, it had no precedent in the New World. Even its legendary date gave it only two centuries. The temples that rose above the houses and the opulent vegetation within the walls belonged mostly to the Tenayuca type, with a reduced number of substructure profiles in the façade design, and the mansard section of the roof of the temple at the same angle of pitch as the sides of the *teocalli.* This is the master stroke of design that makes it seem that Aztec insight was on the way from the colossal in its most vulgar aspect to the monumental. The shrine itself was repeated in two structures on the top of the *teocalli,* and before each shrine was a formal stair leading to the altar of the sacrifice before the fane. In each fane there stood, among other palladia, the image of the divinity. To judge from surviving evidences of sculpture, these images were an arrangement of fear-symbols architecturalized into anthropoid aggregates. This façade is a Chichimec

Plate XXVIII   Santo Domingo Oaxaca, Oaxaca. Façade, central panel.

mode the Aztecs had inherited from their mentors and allies, and it had Toltec antecedents.

The factor of the appearance, however small, of monumentality is significant. Monumentality has little to do with size, little to do with the colossal. It is concerned with the discovery in design of an aspect of power secured by adjusting ratio. As an achievement in design, it is electrifying to the beholder. It is not merely simplification. That can come later, when the adjustments have made for a greater cohesion.

When authentic monumentality may appear, the myth, the symbols, the style and all other related components are near conjunction. There is here, then, the immense potential in liturgical drama and the accoutrements, in music and literary form. In the Aztec situation, the supreme in drama preceded many other possibilities, for one can hardly go beyond human death for drama in the divine liturgy. It would seem, from Spanish descriptions, that its value was the raw effect of the immediacy of the art, since the prana lies in the freshness of the blood and the still-moving heart. There is not much time for temporal aesthetic distance in an abattoir, and a wait would have deprived the God of what He was in need of most — the immediate transfer of strength.

It is moreover a symbolic elaboration, this monumentality, of the time when the gods of one cultural contact in the form of water and fertility deities under the Feathered Serpent were joined with other elements with the Hero of the myth, the Venus symbol related to Mixcoatl. This is the Toltec archetypal situation. It is, naturally, entirely syncretic, and gloriously so, but to us confusing, for our

56

Plate XXVIII-A   Santo Domingo, Oaxaca, Oaxaca.

minds do not dwell upon gods in the interweave of their simultaneous affairs or parallel mythologies. The archetypal situation reminds us of Egypt: Osiris reigns, and too, reigns Ra.

It is Egyptian again in its syncretic character, where figures of the old classical Apollo and Hermes have been transfigured into the Great Apollo and the Great Hermes, the Hellenistic eternal and the universal instead of the Hellenic near and now, and have become Persons, in the coming god sense of the great star times, when Mithras and the Angel of Great Counsel were drawing near. Zeus Serapis comes to mind, the dynastic Great All-Father conjoined into the Apis cult, a mode of Osiris.

For here in Tenochtitlan, the Rain God is joined to a modality of Tezcatlipoca, the divine Tenochca counsellor, Huitzilopochtli. The great temple is oriented on the line of the setting sun, a liturgical practice established hundreds of years before, at Teotihuacan, long buried. Again the cult of Huitzilopochtli is joined to that of Tonatiuh, the Sun in abstract archetype; he becomes the Universal Sun in the now blue sky, and his role as a war-god, too, is augmented. Thus, in its Aztec phase, the Tlaloc theogamy contains the Cloud Serpent, bringer of abundance from the East, the source of rains. By the means of this, Mixcoatl, paternal Hero of the Migrations, deified by his son, shares a shrine on the top of the Great Temple at Tenochtitlan.

And, like the apotheosis of Mixcoatl, almost all the history of the rise of the Aztecs is the story of one more group of the barbarians. For it was these people, and they alone, who produced the art the Spaniards saw. They saw nothing of the art of Mexico's great period,

57

Plate XXIX   Santo Domingo, San Cristóbal de las Casas, Chiapas.

the cities and times and works of Teotihuacan, explored a half a
millenium later.

What the barbarians in an area of ancient cultures do with their
acquisitions is a matter of great interest. It is all the more of interest
in this case. For there was to be an extremely active floration —
pronounced in character, vivid in form — when the barbarian
course is over, and Iberian derivations become, outwardly, the way
of art. What is going to happen when ancient energies in Mexicans,
ruled by the barbarians, come up through the total Toltec and Chichimec overlay, to take form in romanesque, gothic, mannerist,
Islamic modes in re-flattened Andalusian baroque!

Already the shrine on the top of the *teocalli* that was only a hut
as recently as the Xochimilco War, has become, for the Aztec ecclesia, the Metropolitana. The tendency to break down natural form
for ancient ways of showing arcane power in divine animal fear
symbols has appeared, to become a basic direction of style in Aztec
sculpture. This is a style that, among other characteristics, is satis-
fied very often with summations. Late civilization folk have less
time for effective art, and what has to be said is not bound to forms
that are factually or visually descriptive. The time when art of great
inwardness was to be taken for granted has been over for centuries.
Great and poignant inwardness appears at rare times in Aztec sculpture. Summations of some kind may be given to what seems to be
beautiful. In the Aztec tradition, cult sculpture, like the Coatlicue
image of the Mother of the Gods, is an architecturalized assemblage of iconographic elements, with the three-faceted head made
of simultaneous images (a very ancient device of religious art)

Plate XXX   Hacienda Chapel, Vista Hermosa, Morelos.
              Elementary *estipites*.

frightful in hypnotic power of the crotalus, the theme of which Aztec power never tires. So, too, the studied resources of non-naturalistic form are with the same knowledge, insight and assurance set forth in the sculptured serpents, the famous red granite grasshopper, and the architecturalized squash. These things are some of the really great treasures of the Mexican State of the art of its Aztec period. They are free from the total vulgarity of any possible naturalism, even remotely, and they make you pause, dead in your tracks, when you first see them. They are pure thought, pure power, pure essence, free from the incidence of actual form. The Platonic universal has appeared, and no imitation of one imitation is involved here.

One would again here remember Spengler's profound aphorism about human history being without meaning. That the Aztecs should, let us say, suddenly grow so old with such power in art that you look abroad for equivalents in vain, hardly even in late Shang bronzes or earlier Egyptian *Ka* portraits, and then it should all come to an end! It is not this art that emerges again in the glittering domes of the Valley of Puebla, but an art, it seems, of far earlier times.

It might be that it will emerge against itself in the future. Neither the art of modern Mexican architecture, nor the painting nor the sculpture carries any of this strength. The strength of even the later Aztec sculpture reduces all modern Mexican art to pusillanimous emptiness.

In their own overt life, the Aztecs were moving into the political equivalence of this same significance that they had in art, as one may say, blow by blow. Not without poignancy does one feel the

59

Plate XXXI   *Sagrario,* Metropolitana, Mexico, Distrito Federal. Churrigueresque *estipites.*

history grow. The genesis (and involvement) of the dynasts and pantheon has the hope to establish the place in the time picture, even to later political devices of marriage into lineages that had this identity long ago.

The king of Culhuacan who gave the Tizapan site to the Aztecs performed an important step in this history. The first Aztec king, Acamapichtli, claimed descent from these Toltecs of Culhuacan.[27] Marriages into the ruling house of the west shore of Lake Texcoco became policy. Descent is traced through Xolotl of the Toltec Dynasty of Quetzalcoatl of Tula. There are alliances developed from these relationships, and one alliance with the kings of Texcoco and Tacuba makes it possible to invest the Chichimec capital at Azca-potzalco. By this time, it is nearly mid-fifteenth century, and control for the Aztecs extends to South Mexico and into Central America, and they have in all two score garrison-held political appendages that pay tribute, whose people carry it to the capital on their own backs and are themselves held for sacrifice.

The pantheon grows. Huitzilopochtli relates to the blue Tezcat-lipoca of the South, and thus the paleolithic counselor of the wanderings of the hunters takes his place in the direction mandala, inherited ultimately, it is just possible, from generic Siberian antecedents of color traits. Wind and life reside in the West in terms of yellow and white. The Black Tezcatlipoca is in the North. The Red Tezcatlipoca of the East is known under the southern connota-

60

[27] Ignacio Bernal, *Mexico Before Cortez,* p. 98.

Plate XXXII   *Sagrario,* Metropolitana, Mexico, Distrito Federal.
Façade doorway.

tion of Xife. The coalescence going on in the real world begins,
sometimes, to take on a clearer form. This particular historical process has had a long story, but moves on rapidly. As personifications
multiply, the control concepts become remote, and the figures of
immolations of light, of fear, of power are clearly headed toward
some kind of syncretic as well as pantheistic logos. Fusions of fan-
tastic elements and forms are to be found in the attempt to combine
the practical and the aesthetic, to achieve through joining forms the
greatest usefulness with the greatest beauty. Here in Anáhuac, the
rich associations make it necessary to do this by crowding iconographic elements. The Mother of the Gods, a most frightful iconographic agglomeration at first, can in these terms finally be seen
as a beautiful and effective evocation of the intention.

Useful it is to suggest, also, that the Aztecs were not merely
working over the cultural debris of the lake cities, and regions like
Cholula, or the stripped remains of an earlier Anáhuac culture.
Writing in pictographs, with advance into phonetics imminent, was
widely practiced in effective archival resources. It came to the
early Aztecs from Chichimecs returning from Mixtec contacts, and
metal from these same craftsmen appeared at the same time.

Without the prognostication of disaster that obtained particu-
larly at the end of the then current cycle, the outlook could have
been promising it the prevailing rain-securing liturgical formulae
were transcended. It would need the radical departure that religion
is sometimes able to envisage to break the value of the liturgical
sacrifice, as the covenant for rain needed to support a typical neolithic one-crop economy.

They were no worse off than we are, for one-crop economies have been the outstanding, death-demanding curse of modern life, fastening in addition weaknesses from malnutrition on millions the world around, in Europe, Africa, Asia, Puerto Rico, Mexico, the American South, Russia and, of course, in modern Mexico not least.

A few more years and their own solutions might have appeared. But this would have to break through the rigid inexorable traditions of long mnemonic discipline in formal education. It would have, also, to affect the fabric, the whole fabric of the established order. Few societies care that much to survive.

As it was, this world crumbled before early baroque techniques — extension in statecraft, and the various skills at hand to any Spaniard. The extension in statecraft the Aztecs had just discovered for themselves. But Alexander's phalanx made up of the cohesion of Spanish pikemen on the causeway, the dome floating in light far above the piers — these things they could not have imagined. For they had not had even the bow and arrow for very long, as such things go. And even the use of the wheel lay far in the future for them.

THE RICH SOIL for the continued
art after the Conquest of the New World is, as has been suggested,
art from the earlier forms clear through to the Teotihuacan painting
and sculpture, the scripts of the Maya, and of the later cultures in
the Valley of Mexico.

It could be maintained that the temple described as E-VII-sub
at Uaxactún is significant because it is the earliest authentic building now known in that area. Intrinsically, its elaborate fear symbols
and the pattern of stairs make it an advanced work in the early
culture period. In plan, on acount of its projections, it is an already
eight-sided figure.

When we come to examine the building done by the religious
groups of Spain in the New World, we find something of the same
general situation. For nothing is *de novo* in any strict sense. The
single nave church is the form that is to go through a development.
As it happens, the early building of this kind in Spain belongs to
the same decade in which the Reverend Fabric of San Pietro in
Vaticano was started — 1510. There grew up, too, in the New World
a single nave church with aisles going through the heavy lateral
buttress of the nave, or having chapels between the buttresses.
Santo Domingo in Oaxaca is an example of the first kind. This type
of design, worked out mostly in the sixteenth century in Spain, was
important to the Mexican tradition because its decorative statement

4

was made of elements verging toward the gothic, in the use of ribbing, bosses, and some other elements that are seen frequently in these earlier churches in Mexico.

To the visitor from the United States, many questions occur at once about these churches. The immense scale is a cause for dismay; they overwhelm.

Where visitors from North America are accustomed to the colossal and its fatuity, they find in these buildings monumental works of conviction. There is little of the colossal in Mexico, save in the modern period. In the classic period, the defects in the Sun Temple at Teotihuacan show that the classic culture had, in its protruding dikes, come to terms with itself, and was not able to make its symbols to be larger. Anyone who has looked back, when on the highest plane of this structure, to see how the human world disappears at the edge of the plane, with recall the feeling of poignant desolation that obtains. In these churches, one sees monumental power, articulate in similar quality of religious awe, qualities that are alien to size for its own sake.

In the first consideration, this Spanish monumental assurance has to do with faith. Faith gives substance to hope. As a place for worship, churches of these great and noble proportions would encourage neither doubt nor fallibility. There are here alien nations to persuade, and all right means have to be used to do it. To those who crowd in at the North Door, the catechumens' entrance, the grandeur of the proportions they see within is itself miraculous to them, more especially, perhaps, because they themselves had helped to build it. For corporate worship, an old usage that the

64

Plate XXXII-A   *Sagrario,* Metropolitana, Mexico, Distrito Federal.

nations now share with the European newcomer, was formerly done mostly in the dance areas before the pyramid; corporate worship now comes to take place in what architects are going to call, after Vignola's time, designed space.

The fact that almost all of the churches in Mexico come to have many of the characteristics of these early Franciscan buildings makes us want to look at the builders themselves. All the religious orders that came to the New World are unique: Jesuits, Augustinians, Dominicans, Franciscans and others are involved in the development of an architecture for their New World.

Of the Franciscans, the power of the architecture that they developed illuminates the training and character of the men and women. They begin to work in the Province of Holy Evangel, the territory east of Mexico City, the province taking its name from the area of their old home in Spain. They spread west and north and south.

In the first place there are the Apostolic Twelve, those holy men who were the first religious group to bring the Faith to Mexico. They are in no wise misnamed; they are an important factor in the external aspect of the *Ecclesia Docens* and of its architectural fabric. You will see their portraits where they kneel around the Cross in their later *convento* at San Francisco Huejotzingo on the Puebla road.

Before their time, an essential matter for us concerns Francis himself. The whole aim of Francis involved a paradox. Francis wanted to live a life of holiness. Holiness is power. It generates spiritual health and expanding ways of well-being and creativeness, so that it becomes not only something that cannot be resisted, but

65

Plate XXXIII   Santa Prisca, Taxco, Guerrero. Façade, left half.

it becomes something that human societies, once they have seen themselves elevated by these benefits, will not live without, so that, in some cultures, the search for holiness sets the whole style of life, even for the mundane side. Aside from Christianity, clear examples are pre-Buddhic India, and Islam. It draws the world up with it when it rises, and the world, once so lifted up, has to be sustained. For some, holiness will perform the sustaining. For Francis, and some of the Companions, holiness was more than enough. But there were, all of a sudden it seemed, others involved; they not only were to be taught, but they had also to be cared for. It could be said that Francis was himself not too clear how this might be brought about.

The conciliar decision eventually was that the Franciscan Order should divide. The Friars Minor Conventuals take up the responsibility of the worldly contacts, and they administer the Basilica of the Order of Assisi, and follow Pope Urban VIII's decision about property. The group given over to the quest for holiness on the original Franciscan constitution are called Friars Minor Observants — *Observantes* as henceforth noted. The *Observantes* formed in distinct groups in Western Europe. In later times these groups, now autonomous under their Minister-General, contended for the privilege of greater austerities in their discipline. Pertaining to Mexico are, among others, the Recollects, an extreme phase of the *Observantia* founded in France at the end of the sixteenth century. Though of lesser renown, this group participated in the evangelization of the New World. Their gigantic earthquake ruins at Antigua in Gua-

Plate XXXIV   Santa Prisca, Taxco, Guerrero. Doorway.

temala give rise to a vision of something like a Miltonic cataclysm in the architecture of Fourth Dynasty Egypt.

All over the Christian world there was a burgeoning apprehension that moved all the Mendicant Orders, toward the end of the fifteenth century, to self-searching and to reorganization in the public direction of greater singleness of intention and labor. The *Observantes*, by 1517, emerged strong in Spain. A short statement of this growth is very useful for our view of the Mendicant Orders in the New World. The introductory chapter in George Kubler's *Mexican Architecture of the Sixteenth Century*[28] gives a more complete view of them. It is the source of all the statements given here about the Franciscan Mission in Mexico.

It takes us back some thirty years. The group from which the Apostolic Twelve came was called the Minorites of Blessed John of Puebla. This group was formed in 1487, seven years after John of Puebla had joined the *Observantes,* coming from the contemplatives, the Hermits of St. Jerome, in 1480. He organized a new reform when he returned to Spain called the *Custodia de los Angeles,* securing permission for this organization from the General Chapter of the *Observantes* which was held in 1489 in Touraine. Two houses were founded, one near Hornachuelos in the Sierra Morena of Andalusia, called Santa María de los Angeles, in 1490, and the other in 1493 to the north, at Belalcázar, where Blessed John died in 1495. The mission territory the friars wanted was among

[28] George Kubler, *Mexican Architecture of the Sixteenth Century*, I, pp. 1-21.

Plate XXXV   San Francisco, Mexico, Distrito Federal. Lateral entrance.

the Moslem peasants in the northern part of Andalusia. There had been for this area no clergy for a long time. The *Observantes* carried along more emphasis on retreat, and for discipline were nearer to that of Francis. The *Custodia* grew to contain fourteen houses, and it was incorporated in 1518 as the Provincia de los Angeles. Shortly after the death of John of Puebla one of his disciples, Juan de Guadalupe, who wanted to extend the work of the Province to Granada, reorganized this tradition into the Discalced or Barefoot movement, the *Observantia Strictissima,* from which the Capuchin Order was later formed in 1525.

These men were called the Minorites of the Holy Gospel. The Minorites in 1496 won their release from the *Observantes.* They started on a mission to the Moslems of Granada. In this they were, in dealing with an alien folk and an alien language, preparing for the great evangelical mission that was to be theirs in 1523 in America.

The number of recruits that went into the *Observantia Strictissima* alarmed the older reformed Order and by 1502 these *Observantes* were able to secure a brief from the Pope, Alexander VI, revoking the privileges which he had granted the *Strictissima* in 1496. For a time the *Observantes Strictissima* went into forced exile in Portugal. They later, upon their return, found their old houses, Trujillo and Salvaleon, in ruins. Again they met persecution from the *Observantes* because, in order to escape trouble from the *Observantes,* they had given their allegiance to the Conventuals. The *Strictissima* were raised to the status of a province by Julius II, in 1508, with the *Custodia* of la Piedad in Portugal and that of Santo Evangelio in Castile. The Chapter General of the Franciscans then

Plate XXXVI   La Compañía, Guanajuato, Guanajuato. Façade.

persuaded them to join the Franciscan Order. The Portuguese province joined the *Observantes* and the Castilian province remained with the Conventuals.

Under Leo X, the various reform groups of the Franciscan Order were once again asked to join it. The Piedad and the Santo Evangelio were given provincial status and both joined the *Observantes.* The Castilian province was renamed San Gabriel. Meanwhile the followers of John of Puebla had formed a third province called Nuestra Señora de los Angeles.

These missions and retreats did not attract the *Observantes* and the Conventuals. The followers of John of Puebla adopted the name of the Castilian custody of 1517, the Santo Evangelio, when naming their Mexican mission territory. The *Strictissima* had a clearly defined status as apostolic preachers. These Franciscans worked in the communities of Andalusian farmers which had been neglected, and secured in this way the preparation for the work in America that the Conventuals and the Regular Observants had been unwilling to do. It is to be noted that here they were working with non-European folk (Moslem peasants), as they would be in the New World, preaching there at first to Totonacs of various kinds, to Otomí, to Tlaxcalans from the first days.

The Cardinal de Santa Cruz probably worked out the plan for the Apostolic Twelve. He had been a General of the Order, and he himself wished to go to the New World. Leo X gave him permission to do so on April 25, 1521. But being a Franciscan, he could not deal with Charles V on the Holy See on an Erasmian basis. He did expect, with the pre-Reformation views of Cardinal Cisneros,

69

Plate XXXVII   La Compañía, Guanajuato, Guanajuato. Façade.

that the piety of the age might be revived through the strict Franciscan Observance.

The order was given by Cardinal de Santa Cruz in 1523 to start for America. It was given to Martín de Valencia, at a chapter meeting at San Gabriel at Belvis in Castile. He draw his men from among the one hundred and seventy-five men in eleven houses of the Province. All of these men had sought out the *Strictissima* from the more lax discipline of other Conventual establishments. Some. of these men had considered joining the Carthusians. "It was a tightly knit, radical little band of men who had worked together for many years as apostolic preachers and in the intention of effecting great conversions."[29] The first Bishop of Mexico was Juan de Zumárraga, a Franciscan. He was appointed bishop in 1527. By 1525, the *Philosophia Christi* of Erasmus was well known in Spain. It is strongly surmised that Zumárraga intended to make use of this work in teaching the Indians, after 1540.

Zumárraga was concerned with the diffusion of scripture, the rejection of scholasticism, and the doctrine of interim Christianity. One finds in Zumárraga's adaptations the intention of faith over works. This Lutheranism — from Seville — had wide publication in Spain.

With these indications of what was happening at the reform level in Spain — the ferment, the anguish for more intense austerity, the insistence, the rejection, the dedication — it is not surprising that, in the subsequent intense apprehension of the reform, there was

[29] George Kubler, *Mexican Architecture of the Sixteenth Century*, I, p. 8.

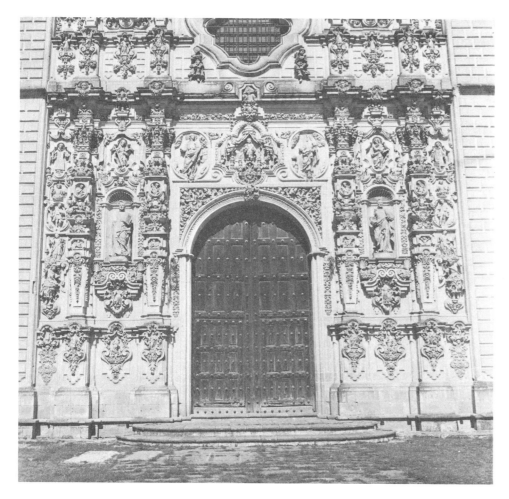

Plate XXXVIII   San Martín Tepotzotlán, Mexico. Façade.

violence after the General Chapter of the Regular Observance at Toulouse in 1530. Later, in Mexico, Vasco de Quiroga and others, aided by Court influence, carried on the social application of ideas of the later reforms in plans for Indian resettlements.

The men under whom the early building in Mexico took place were thus persons of unique selection and apostolic power. The divine commission to go forth to preach was carried out by the earlier Twelve Apostles after their grief and disillusionment had given them insight. In their authority they spread quickly over the whole world. The legend, as it is beautifully set forth by Hugo van der Goes in his painting, "The Falling Asleep of the Virgin," in the Musée Communal in Bruges, has them all returned, some even from America and India. These are the men whom it is not so easy to recognize in the fourteenth chapter of the Gospel of St. John. These had to be persuaded once more, after infinite revelation. On the other hand, these men of western Europe, Spaniards, some Frenchmen and Flemish, had the revelation of their inwardness in piety, and its creative action, just as their Master had told them to do, to "believe me for the very works' sake." A part of their world mission is treated of in these descriptions. For the architecture they set up, and the growth of style they afforded, is an expression of this power.

They soon affected the landscape of Mexico. Eventually, a view without a dome, a tower, may be judged to be hardly characteristic. And then, the town itself is mostly a new idea, demographically. Indigenous New World towns were not entities in the European sense, legal units, but rather they were aggregates with deliberately

Plate XXXIX   San Martín Tepotzotlán, Mexico. Façade, upper storey.

diffused forms that floated and shifted slowly, in most typical examples, around a ceremonial center. The comparison, if any, is not to walled Avila or Florence, but rather to the old Kremlin, with the formless "Kitaegorod" around it. Towns like Tlaxcala and Yanhuitlan are fresh exceptions, made to order by the new order in Mexican society.

In the middle stands high and greater in scale the Church, looking deceptively at first as though it had military uses. The great block of it dominates everything in the landscape; it shakes with the assurance of power — Actopan, Ixmiquilpan — and around lies the grid of the town, dusty in mild sufferance and shadowy form. But in the midst, is the reality. The great bloc has one thing to say to the old order, and to the new order, and it says it, with Mosaic power and finality: *Credo in Unum Deum.*

Once this has been said in the ratio of thick wall, high ceiling, perfectly extended breadth and length, the tired, old, long-abandoned ruins gave up what was left of their ghost. Teotihuacan, Xochicalco, Calixtlahuaca, Monte Albán and the synthetic resuscitations of the Chichimec — Cholula and Tenochtitlan — now seem far away and long ago. The structure at Teotihuacan, the "Sun" Temple, had the highest substructure set fatally back from the top edge of the one beneath it. Just a few feet as the sacrifice walked toward the last substructure stair: and now, well-lost indeed, the whole world was fallen below the architectural horizon, invisible, henceforth, clear on up to the top. This ninth century structure is probably the peak of architectural inwardness in New World ritual architecture, and perhaps the end of it. For it is not clear

72

Plate XL   Santo Domingo, Oaxaca. Main cloister and façade towers.

that it was understood at Cholula, and there is no reason to suppose that it was understood at Tenochtitlán. For there the emphasis seems not to have been on sacrifice as a gift, though George Vaillant asserts that this is not unknown, but rather on the implacable hunger of Huitzilopochtli. Once these churches, the new structures in the new towns brought another world into being, the old order lost most of its already aged power, and soon lost most dependable memory. Morley made a strong point of the complete loss even of old place names in Mesoamerica.

Such a trend could partly follow the forgetfulness about the old order. The polarity of the old order was not *caritas* but malevolence at the heart of its divine world. In the Maya world the weight of the practice of the temporal considerations becomes hard to carry, as small units of time take symbols. Responsibility in the modes of fear come to signify the determined polity of an ecology based on blood gift in terms of quantity as well as quality imputed in this god-substance. Prana, at least, may not be palliated. And what is in store for a priesthood that cannot guarantee rain for the one-crop economy of grain?

Aside from the insight of their views of this demonology, as they thought of Mesoamerican religion, the Franciscans and their monastic confrères had motives that produced growth in power in most activities. It is consonant to their directness in style that their work in architecture is not without recollection of the churches without side aisles in romanesque Spain and France. These churches recall the buildings without transepts used for the liturgy in earlier times. The bloc that looms above Atlixco and Tlatelolco

Plate XLI   Cathedral, Saltillo, Coahuila. Façade, regional baroque.

and Tepeyaca says the word that is to be the fiat of the new order. In any impact of cultures, there is disaster, chaos, pain, confusion, hunger, disease, despair, and death, some here, some there. But with quiet eventuality, a new order was soon apparent.

The beginning of the art is in the vigor of the architecture. It is a part of the whole picture that there was no architecture in the old order. A corbel-arch *posa* on the top of a series of truncated substructures is not architecture in the coming sense of the word. It may be very wonderful theatre for the heaven-world, from which the gods watch the dance that is so important in corporate worship. But architecture as the design of space is coming to be the view of the world of this building tradition, in these very decades when it was being transplanted to the New World.

The Mendicant formula of architectural proportion was amenable to manipulation on a very large scale. The secular church, managed mostly on the proportions of the Gesù in Rome, allowed for the variety of floor plans that came in at the end of the sixteenth century, with the closing of the vicariates apostolic. But these new taut single nave churches of the Mendicants state a singleness of form that shows, in exalted clarity, a passion of purpose.

We may now come back to this structure as it stands, often, in the middle of the new town. The town itself is something of a literary creation, largely, of Italian writers like Leone Battista Alberti (1404-1472; *De re aedificatura,* 1485). The planned town had little precedent in Italy, and none in Spain; it was a renaissance gift to the New World.

Few places anywhere have the delightful arrangement of La

Plate XLII   Chapel, Tepeyac, above the Basilica at Guadalupe, Distrito Federal.

Soledad, Our Lady of Sorrows, in Oaxaca. It is not a palatial location at all. It is purely urban expression, of grand stairs, park, trees, a large Moorish-type fountain, atria, two convents, chapel, and a basilica with a great sculptured façade three stories high. In the great enframement over the main entrance, Our Lady of Sorrows is contemplating the prime symbol of mortality — the skull at the foot of the Cross.

This wonderful square is a later usage and an elaborate one, made complicated by a steep hillside site. Other churches in Antequera have parks in front of them, or nearby, or long beside the consecrated walled area, or within the atrium, like the trees and fountains on the epistle side at Carmen Alto.

But for the early sixteenth century single nave churches, the park is apt to be some indication between the front outer wall of the atrium and the town itself. Actopan with its shrivelled dusty little town has a row of new planted saplings leading to the gate itself. But the monumental Augustinian establishment rises like a massif behind it. The grounds iside the atrium may be an attractive place of repose, like the one at Carmen Alto in Oaxaca, or at Ixmiquilpan where the park, as used to happen, was also a cemetery, as well as an orchard garden as at Huejotzingo. It has been said that man was lost in a garden, and redeemed in one. A cemetery within a church, or near to one, will be near also to the soul-saving *Pneuma* of the Holy Ghost.

It is of Santiago de Tlatelolco that there is a first illustration. One is to imagine it without the classical detail of a renaissance doorway. The massive corner buttresses are what one sees first.

Plate XLIII   House in Querétaro, Querétaro.

Then one sees the variegated texture of the color of the outside walls. As historians we are interested in this great stark block first. (Plate II.) Here on the site of the great pyramid of Tlatelolco, and made partly of its stone, the *Observantes* put up one of the earliest churches. The first one was built on the platform of the Aztec market, the very place where Father Bernardino de Sahagún used to take notes. The first structure was a church of three aisles. The church shown in the picture is not the earliest one, but one made at a later time. In this collection of illustrations there is no other picture that shows the element of texture so well.

There is a sense, it might be said, in which Mexicans think and feel in stone. In neolithic times the great works were undertaken in stone and brick. The Iberian invasion enriched the techniques immeasurably. Yet one must train oneself, in living in Mexico, to surmise that in this matter the old order is never replaced. In many regions the evidence is all about. Stone and materials relating to it are everywhere, in constant use, in constant re-use. It is a trait. It is almost unimaginable in North America.

One is not in the presence of this trait very long before he becomes aware that stone is also used for color. In Oaxaca I have seen workmen take long to work out the appearance of a retaining wall for a large garden. Choosing, reflecting, selecting again, they worked until the right sizes, colors and shapes were in place. This wall was torn down the next morning, and rebuilt to the greater satisfaction of the workmen. Here it should be remembered that color in stone is also a strong Mediterranean trait, and here the two traits, not identical in operation, but one ancient and strong in

Plate XLIV   Organ, Metropolitana, Mexico, Distrito Federal.
Coro, altar end.

the Mediterranean world and one ancient in the New World, flow together, contributing eventually to most opulent results.

As far as texture is concerned, it can be seen in Plates II, III, IV, and V. Color in this volcanic stone ranges from a deep purple of low intensity and low color value through to an extremely red range of low intensity and low color value. In Plate IV one can see the ashlar variations. The vertical three stage doorway may be seen in contrast to later forms in Plates XVII and XVIII. The austerity of the mass of the building is apparent. But many other structures of an earlier date show this austerity and monumentality better. There was no wavering to get a similar effect in the interior. There was no wavering of complete liturgical singleness in the interior, except at Zimapan, where there is elaborate architectural provision, unique so far as one knows, for the celebration of many eucharistic dramas at the same time.

A while back we were looking at these earlier churches trying to estimate the significance of these great blocs, in a religious landscape where corporate worship had been so entirely out of doors. Considerations of design had been based on the horizontals. This is noted everywhere, but it is shown clearly in the long lines of the Quetzalcoatl complex at San Juan Teotihuacan. It is emphasized in the top edge of the substructures, one above the other, the more clearly in the Mexican type of pyramid temple base.

In Plate VI, the façade of Santo Domingo Yanhuitlan, is shown the power of the verticals in the planning of elaborate design. The concentration of horizontals and verticals between the tower buttresses, a later addition to this façade, accentuate the problem,

Plate XLIV-A Metropolitana, Mexico, Distrito Federal. Detail of altar.

with a somewhat restraining effect of the architrave courses and their heavy undulating shadow. It looks as if these taut shadows were giving way to verticalization expressed in the pilasters.

The crest of the vault ribbing inside is very nearly as high as the gable, seen in the façade; the processional drive toward the altar seems indeed forcibly expressed. The force of the drive seems to come from the great height of the round windowless apse. It is not done so effectively in the Metropolitana. The height and the distance are there, but the nave with the *coro,* and the altar liturgically polar to this *coro,* get in the way.

In Plate VI the great buttress on the gospel side pairs with the rear one. They were erected at the end of the sixteenth century when the weight of the high thick stone, especially the enormous blocks of the parapet, was excessive for the somewhat soft stone. In weather and time this stone takes on much of the beautiful ranges of color tones of yellows, gold, rose and cerise that one sees on the inside of the cave at Be-ta-ta-Kin in the Segi Canyons in northeastern Arizona.

The open tower is made of the flat Roman brick the Spaniards brought to the New World. There is a tile dome on it. The support for the epistle side comes from the conventual buildings, and in the first cloister the great cedar can be seen by the tower.

All of Santo Domingo Yanhuitlan is built on a slope. The retaining wall is about one hundred feet behind the round apse. Below the wall is the city park; around the park is the town. The extent of the atrium can be seen in Plate I. Its wall is far to the

Plate XLV   Kabah, Yucatán. Puuc manner, façade.

right. The immense field is like the one at San Francisco at Cholula, the preaching field for the catechumens.

The Dominican Order had plans for the town at Cuilapan, moving streams in the mountains, setting up a mill. Like Santo Domingo Yanhuitlan, Santo Domingo Cuilapan has little of the town left around it now. It was not until after some of these settlements were made that the population drift to the northeast was apprehended. Dominicans are practical people. They would never have built greater than their present need would have indicated. The barns themselves are immense; the scale would have been large for elephants. This impression is emphasized in the scale of the uncompleted choir and the bay underneath the choir, where the great supporting ribs rest on consoles. The long low basilica in the left side of Plate VII does not belong to the first plan. In the rear, there is a grand archway leading into the conventual church, to the ruined bay in front of the choir bay.

When one enters these early churches the vision is drawn upward to the ceiling. In many of the earlier churches the ceiling in the half-dome over the altar (that is, where there is a semicircular apse) will often have an elaborate vaulting held up by ribs. The bay in front of the half-dome may have somewhat the same vaulting pattern. Some of the Franciscan churches have rib vault for the whole of the nave. Many Dominican churches have vaulting for the sanctuary and the one bay in front of it. The rest of the nave may have a long, usually quite unrelieved barrel vault. The Augustinian churches have something of the same form. At Tepeaca

Plate XLVI   Kabah, Yucatán. Puuc manner, section.

(Plate VIII) the simple vaulting form can be seen. In the farther bay one may see the masonry, where it is revealed in areas from which the surface plaster has fallen. Thus one may see how the masonry is supported by the ribs.

At Ixmiquilpan (Plate IX), an Augustinian household, the rib pattern is more elaborate. At Acolman the ceiling masonry is made up of larger blocks, and they seem to be supporting the sanctuary dome resting on the circumference of the apse wall. Here, where much of the ceiling decoration has fallen away, it looks as if the ribbing were a secondary consideration, and that the vaulting is really self-sufficient. This may be so, to some extent. The concrete plaster which is used is hard, as good a building material as much of the stone that is employed, so that over all the ribbing structure and the dome structure it makes a hard shell for the roof, the whole of it, ribbing, stone vaulting and concrete being lighter than the heavy, thick walls. All these matters are developments of the late gothic usages in Western Europe.

Another matter that looks back through a long perspective of development in Europe is the nature of the vaulting as space design. Where it is groin vaulting, as in the second bay at Acolman and in the vaults you can see in Plates VIII or IX, one element seems to keep them somewhat near much of the old romanesque pattern of form. That is, the level of the transverse ribs is a good deal lower than the crossing of the diagonal ribs. The effect, then, of height was managed by many factors; many, like this one, somewhat adventitious. Then, there usually was no regular arrangement of windows — one opposite another — the areas of light and dark made

Plate XLVII   Mitla, Oaxaca. Main quadrangle, wall section.

their own rhythm. They interrupted what often would have been a heavy regularity, and effect visual results of height and distance. This can be guessed at in Plate IX, for in this gigantic Augustinian nave, the floor is a long way down, indeed, something like eighty feet.

The time has come now to take a general glance at this first group of buildings, the churches of the Mendicant Orders, of the Franciscans, the Dominicans and the Augustinians, in the time from 1530 to about 1580 or 1600. When we have shown that the proportions of length, breadth and height have an arresting effect of monumentality that is the clear diction, here, of religious awe, we have described a great matter, the great matter of the Mexican style. To see these buildings as ornament, as over against the stable form of the house, is to see them in their essential light. For these buildings belong to the taboo side of the social structure, to those things that are set aside and are of an exclusive reserve in social usage, as over against the totemic consideration of things that belong to the clan and its symbol.

In the sense then that the totemic side is the stable family succession and its affairs, its buildings never change their essential form, so that the farmstead can move to the palace, and decline someday back to the garth and never lose its essential early parts.

Buildings of the taboo side are in their very nature indeed quite the opposite. They are ornament, in size, monumentality, function and availability to growth and change of given form, in which role they are the vehicle of style. Here it is the ornamental side that is the expression of the piety of the culture; as far as the culture is considered, its history in form is in the complete story of the

Plate XLVII-A   Mitla, Oaxaca. Temple and church.

architecture when one discusses these matters in terms of architecture as we do here in Mexico. This story can be told in other ways, too, and behind architecture is religion and its uses of ornaments. Religion itself is the ornament of the society, for it is concerned with the most important thing that some societies have; that is growth. The being side is the house, the becoming side is the altar. The events in form for societies that face the challenge of a possible growth, as only some do, are the Castle and the Cathedral.

We could with immense interest look into the Castle and the Cathedral as they loom over the scattered non-urban folk in pre-Cortesian time, and one has only to bring into his recollection the staggering escarpment at Tikal, with its lakes where hundred-foot trees now stand, their tops where water once carried boats past ecclesiastical palaces along the Main Plaza, with the South Acropolis structures mirrored in the waters. The North Acropolis with its pyramids rising in tiers, their crests and combs as in Temple II, catching the sunlight, like Chephren's *ben-ben,* long before it reaches the far-lying villages below. Here the situation is a more normal one, in a way, for there is something immensely attractive to people burdened with the costs of later civilization, like long-range weapons, in viewing the time when Church and State were one, and the Cathedral was the Castle also, as it might, for the times, be said.

It is part of the wrench that Mexicans had to endure that their share of this pre-Cortesian picture was moving rapidly toward its end in the Aztec floration. When the Iberians set up their patterns

Plate XLVII-B   Mitla, Oaxaca. Temple, patterned tepics.

of one merged often in the function of the other. Hence, it is no great mystery, and should be no occasion for surprise, when we find that audience for the Apostle to the Indians (Las Casas' later title) is at the Hapsburg Court. The Orders were involved too near the scene to act in agreement. The Cathedral side, that is, the side of becoming, appears in the New World art in a young or a new pattern. Hence its own ornamental statement is already long developed in its historical background in Portugal, in Spain, in Italy, in France and in Flanders, for it was from so far away, Flanders, that at least one of the earlier Franciscans came, a companion to the Apostolic Fathers mentioned earlier.

It came almost to full bloom in the New World, rich, crowding, progressing until the Orders were soon hard pressed to tell which phase of the style to espouse. The gothic rib-structure we have mentioned. When Tepeaca was begun, the pier bases of the new St. Peter's were twenty years old. When the façade of Yuriria and Acolman were eventually available after 1530, the vernacular of commingled styles, late gothic, renaissance, mudéjar, were already waiting to be planted, to spread, to grow, so that it seems indeed not long before what you can see at Yuriria (Plate XI) and Acolman on the Mexican spiritual landscape, the role of Castle and Cathedral were long established and clear, and so old that the function (Plate XVI), Santa Prisca (Plate XVIII), in Taxco, or the heaven-glimpse in gold and candlelight you see at La Valenciana. (Plate XIX).

Although it has little decoration on it, the church on the hilltop above San Cristóbal de las Casas, in far-away Chiapas, is pure

Plate XLVII-C   Mitla, Oaxaca. Temple, patterned tepics.

ornament. If, when you look at it in Plate X, you understand this statement, then you will see that the covering of these buildings, on the outside and on the inside, with the vernacular of the progressive styles, carries the symbols of the stylistic system. Eventually, forms that have no meaning at all are used, also to cover walls, almost in the sense of concealing them.

Ornament says something. It is the métier of the spiritual articulation, along with the more essential articulation of dogma and doctrine in liturgies, with texts, in fact, it may for all of our considerations be considered as equipment. Music is needed, and color. So there is, first, the floor plan.

The floor plan is a statement of ornament. On it are built the designed spaces, with walls, windows, vaults, supports and furniture, all themselves covered again, in the fulfillment of style, with symbols in a language powerfully interwoven in associations. The floor plan of the Parthenon indicates a *cella,* a room without windows, originally quite small, and this room has the *pradakshina,* the sacred going around a static sun, arranged for outside in the peristyle. The floor plan of a Christian chuch is a progression in dynamics for ritual contained within the designed space. In the earlier sixteenth century churches in Mexico, the basilica has the preaching field to the front or to the left, that is, north side — the gospel side if the altar faces east. There is a door about the middle of the north side to the field. The conventual buildings are on the right side, the epistle side, of the church as you face the altar. The door in the epistle side gives out to the cloister. Sometimes around the cloister, behind its wall, is a hallway, often an ample hall. The

84

Plate XLVIII   An *artesonada* doorway.

doors to the cells give off from this hall. These cells are often generous rooms with high ceilings, and a window, with a seat in the
thick walls. The stairway of the cloister is often of palatial scale
and palatial grandeur, as at Santo Domingo Yanhuitlan and Santo
Domingo Oaxaca. Continuing out from this cloister there is often
another, and sometimes there is more than one other, the farther
merging into the farm quarters. This general plan is frequent but it
is not arbitrary, and it does not obtain at all in Cuilapan.

The atrium is clearly marked off. Usually there is a wall, often
with formal or monumental gates. This is, in molded brick, a very
impressive gate at San Francisco Acatepec, south of Cholula. In
some of the earlier Mendicant Order sites, when the atrium is not
too large there are corner chapels — the *posas* — that serve proces-
sions as a place to pause for prayers.

At the basilica of Teotitlan del Valle the dedication is to the
Feast of the Most Precious Blood; the procession is led by three
musicians who have pre-Cortesian instruments, walking about thirty
feet ahead of the band. The procession stops with the image, in
this case a painting of the Crucifixion which is the palladium of the
Cult, in the *capilla posa,* in the corner of the atrium, for prayers and
incensation. Such a *capilla posa* (Plate XXI) can be seen at the
Franciscan site of Huejotzingo, en route to Puebla. The vigorous
style of early Christian sculpture in Mexico is seen here. Another
manner of early sculpture can be seen (Plate XX) over a doorway at
Tepoztlan. The crosses, too, like the one at Huejotzingo (Plate
XXII) with its rough texture, show something of the earlier sculpture.

What Professor Wachter calls the Tequitqui Cross in the

85

Plate XLIX   San Francisco Huejotzingo, Puebla.

parroquia at the basilica of Guadalupe (Plate XXIII) is most interesting as iconographic communication in sculpture. It seems like a glimpse of realization taking place in the flames and clashes that mark the course of the impact of the two cultures meeting in early conflict and confusion: autochthonic power, but in Spanish terms. The highest relief on the Cross is the monogram of Pilate's superscription, *Iesus Nazarenus, Rex Iudaeorum,* for it is the emphatic part of the design. The rest of the sculpture is in low relief. Around the letters a kind of *tocado* in the static flamboyance of archaic *putti* heads and wings, the indication of bodilessness of angels. Beneath it in shallow relief, the thorn-crowned head has at the juncture of the arms of the Cross a kind of aureola around it, a great shoulder wreath of a Crown of Thorns.

Here of all places in early Christian Mexico, in a work so non-Iberian in its power and connotation that you expect an Indian countenance might once appear, the chance is significantly surrendered. What is there, rather, is a generalized countenance — sad, silent, utterly vulnerable with a great Visigothic mustache and the divided Castilian beard. Thus in this least Spanish of works the surrender of identity, the most Spanish of all Spanish Christian virtues, pervades the total work; yet in a manner this Cross is easily one of the most "Indian" of all works of sculpture of vicariate times.

One of the elements about it is the lithic character in the large fresh rendition of the Blood, the Nails, the Pillar, the Rope, the Cock, the Lance, the Seamless Robe, then lastly, the witnesses for the created order, the Sun and the Moon. All of the Instruments of the Passion, and some of the witnesses, are there. But the Instru-

Plate L   La Valenciana, Guanajuato, Guanajuato. Altar, and
           sacristy door sculpture.

ments of the Passion are superseded by another kind of sacramental.
It is the stole wrapped around the bloodied Hands, symbolically, with
the divine Feet, represented on the Cross as an interweave of bleed-
ing. It is a profoundly theological touch dominating the rest of the
symbols. For all the great power of the Cross, the stole here is a
deference to the non-Indian side of the design. For neither the
Cross nor the Passion is an end in itself, but they were endured
in order that the Logos might become fulfilled. It is the teaching that
has to be carried forth, started, supported, protected and perpet-
uated. This striking Cross makes the stole a clear sign for the
Church, the *Ecclesia Docens,* the end for which the Cross is a
means. For it is within the faculty of the stole, a credential, that
the Church speaks. The stole is worn at all sacerdotal functions.
It is marked with a cross, and it is addressed with a kiss.

Moreover, this Cross is not just one more work of Mexican art,
like the great Tree of St. Dominic in white and gold in the under-
choir bay at Santo Domingo in Oaxaca. It calls up, in association,
the power of Gislebertus of Autun, a romanesque sculptor who can
communicate in the fear aspect of religious awe. There is the un-
forgettable wordless countenance, and the arms that end in the
flames, so often seen on crosses of all kinds, in Mexico.

The language of ornament on these passages of sculpture de-
velops in statements that are more and more formal. Once started,
it has an interesting history in the churches of the Mendicant Orders.
Then it flares on the outside, the inside, and then the outside again
on the cathedral churches and the domed parish churches of a
somewhat later time.

87

Plate LI   San Agustín Church, Salamanca, Querétaro.
St. Ann altar panel, right side.

We can now leave this interlude between pre-Cortesian art and the art of somewhat autochthonic interlude of the missionary times. With the end of the vicariates, the bishops came. In the missionary epoch, the forms of the church we have touched upon, primal ornament in themselves, became the framework of ornament derived from many sources. They are, at first sight, like the plateresque matters, of strange ancestry indeed. The vernaculars of many times, places, tendencies, and generalizations make up these systems of ornaments.

In this sense the historic order of Mexican style begins its growth with the cathedral times, the last decade or so of the sixteenth century. The work of the Orders contracts. They continue, but do not expand much more. Other Orders, moreover, coming later on the scene, take up the helping of the diocesan clergies. There were never enough of the secular or regular clergy really to address the task of conversion in the New World.

Plates XI, XII, XIII, XIV and XV show the Franciscan house at Yuriria and the Augustinian house at Acolman. The monuments are often described as plateresque. It seems at first to be a modified renaissance design. In Spain the shallow design on metal, usually silver, satisfies a taste that was once widespread. In the early sixteenth century the term was applied to architecture. In the New World it came to be employed when it became a desired thing to cover the space between the towers, in the earlier monastic buildings, with enrichment. The plateresque point of view had taken up rhythmic characteristics that set it apart, or rather ahead of medieval or renaissance rhythms. What was worked out was a way of relating

Plate LII   San Agustín Church, Salamanca, Querétaro.
The Virgin of Guadalupe altar.

the form of the design to the whole space involved. But it is basically an Islamic motivation. It aims to cover the area of the building
spaces on which it is placed. In strict consideration, there is here
a reaching toward an overall pattern. This is a general characteristic of the Islamic point of view. It has a more specific area in the
mudéjar point of view. This is the tradition of building and crafts
practiced by workmen brought up in Moorish Spain — Andalusia,
Granada, Murcia and Valencia — but the influence is not strictly
confined to these regions.

In Spain there was a different history for art from that which
flourished in Western Europe. It is useful to recall that late gothic
had a very long twilight in Spain. One may remember that it continued in the tradition, as renaissance, mannerist, and baroque styles
took root. The ultimate Islamic form of the overall pattern re-
quires no relief; in Islamic works of art it usually has very little. The
elements of the design appear on one plane, and extend, contiguous
and exactly repeated, in all directions on the plane. The sensibility
that is involved, then, is as much for the space that is between the
elements of the design as it is for the design itself. It is not in-
frequent that the space between takes over the whole aspect, and
although the simultaneity is not unknown in other traditions, it is
one of the glories of visual things Islamic, full of surprises and
sudden power and evocative suggestions that connects it with
Mesopotamian — that is, old Mesopotamian — dealings with the Un-
conscious. When this takes place a fresh richness is often the result.
Moreover, the design in many cases moves later out into a third
dimension. The later effect of this tendency will be seen in part

89

Plate LIII   San Agustín Church, Salamanca, Querétaro.
St. Joseph altar, right side.

on the seventeenth and eighteenth century churches. At Acolman and Yuriria, its related establishment, it might make more simple the approach to this problem to say that the basis of the design seems to be the late classical triumphal arch design and its renaissance decoration.

This had come anew into European art in the Florentine tradition, and it was in use as a renaissance convention. There is the round arch over the portal, the elaborate architrave held up by pairs of pilasters on either side; in both of these cases, pilasters in three-quarters relief. These pilasters are ornamental with floral and other patterns in relief. The arch bears a border of coffers in relief, the jambs bear statues in three-quarters relief with architectural canopies. Between the side pilasters in prominent proportions are the two great teachers of the Church, Peter and Paul. Sculptured forms of angels are above the door arch.

The architrave is filled with classical horses, with lions' heads, portraits in rondels and escutcheons. All of these indications are kept somewhat flat, and are used as additional ornament to the wall panel in which the door, at first unadorned, was placed. In finish and virtuosity there are touches all over both doors, of shields hanging from ribbons, shells and trophy forms. But it is in the flat manner of the silversmith's tradition on the whole, and it does not leave the wall as later forms do, with assurance that is confounding.

Before the development of the plateresque in Mexico, in the middle of the sixteenth century, the prevalence of this vernacular can be surmised in the painted decoration of Santiago Tlatelolco (Plate XXIV), although the painting here is older than the façade

Plate LIV   San Agustín Church, Salamanca, Querétaro.
                  St. Joseph altar, right side.

at Acolman (Plate XVI), in the Actopan refectory (Plate XXV), and in the black and white fresco borders of Acolman (Plate XXVI).

FOR OUR purposes of making
a study of style in viceregal architecture we move farther from
the churches of the Mendicant Orders. The interest will be on the
uses of the things architecture employs to say what it is commis-
sioned to say. As we have already seen, this concerns a body of
forms that are in the tradition. They have, in one way or another,
been used for many centuries. Many of the elements in this phase
of tradition come from classical architecture. In classical architecture almost all of the elements at one time or another had been used
in structures. Most histories of architecture will illustrate in its
wooden stage the classical temple. They will illustrate, too, a profound aphorism in art: a form developed in one material and tradition will sometimes carry over into a new structure when it is made
of another material, but in the old form, as far as possible. The
classical temple, then, in moving from wood to cut stone, adapts
to an extent the stone to wood form, and wood to stone form. In
this tradition the old forms take on new meaning when they have
to be made in the new material. They appear without structural
function, but they come to have an exceedingly valuable use in
the new role. Released, they can be made larger and clearer and
appear as the data of an altered aesthetic, perhaps a new one,
and can thereafter be used as a language, as for its own sake.

In Greek architecture the vernacular of ornament appears completely free of structural reference, first in the Choragic Monument of Lysicrates in Athens. The extent to which the released data can go is revealed in the tepidarium of the Baths of Caracalla, where the great hall with its barrel vault and cross vaulting, surely non-classical forms, is completely covered, from vaulting to figured floor, with a wonderfully worked-out system of classical architectural decoration: columns, capitals, floors, architraves, imposts, friezes, coffering patterned of marble in color to cover the walls of structural concrete. This building, groined vault over arches on piers, is in structure an oriental form concealed with classical ornamentation. This is a non-classical trait that subsequent cultures in the West retained down to the twentieth century. "No Corinthian columns!" after hundreds of years, became a criterion for our contemporary architecture. Before that time, this vernacular was used everywhere. The renaissance style, plateresque, the mannerist, the baroque, the churrigueresque, the rococo, the neo-classic all used it, in some ways strangely indeed.

In Mexico, then, we are in the midst of the tradition that has turned up even in India and China, and had been completely introverted in romanesque time. Here it freed itself indeed. When we come to the little viceregal towns, like Taxco or Oaxaca (Plate XXVII), you can, from a distance, see the towers of some of these interesting buildings. In this picture, also, you can see the mounds of the great pre-Cortesian site, Monte Albán, on the crest of the highest hill to the extreme right. The towers of Santo Domingo de Oaxaca you can see at the left of the town. We can take this building as a place

Plate LV   La Valenciana, Guanajuato, Guanajuato,
               San Cayetano, High Altar.

to begin. On Plate XXVIII the decorative arrangement is in deeper
relief than what we saw at Acolman. It rises in four stages. In each
of the first three stages a pair of engaged columns stands on each
side of the central panel. In stage one, they are at the sides of the
door; in stage two, at the sides of the panel of the Donation; in
stage three, at the sides of the window. The horizontals are marked
strongly; the somewhat Corinthian moldings and architecture make
strong shadows that help build up the elevation. At the fourth stage
there is a broken pediment around the coat of arms bearing the
Cross of the Dominican Order. This is in the plateresque style and
in most of the other styles is the basic scheme for manipulation of
light and shadow. On this vertical axis of the central panel, all such
schemes are worked out. In very many cases it will be worked out
further, as it is here, and the paired engaged columns will become
a kind of a unit. Between them there will be one niche, or two, or
maybe more; they will be articulated with shells, consoles, scrolls,
and eventually many other devices. The niches will contain statues,
and the whole will be a frontal presentation of the design of a
retablo, an architecturally decorative background for Dominican
personages often presented as portraits.

If you put Plate XXVIII, Santo Domingo de Oaxaca, and Plate VI,
Santo Domingo Yanhuitlan, side by side, you will see the rich control
of symmetrical shadows and lights and have a basis for understanding the ecstatic enrichment that comes in later examples. It
can be said there are scores of variations of these two façades; the
clue to the reading of them, the kind you have already seen in La
Santisima (Plate XVII), Santa Prisca (Plate XVIII), and in the interior

95

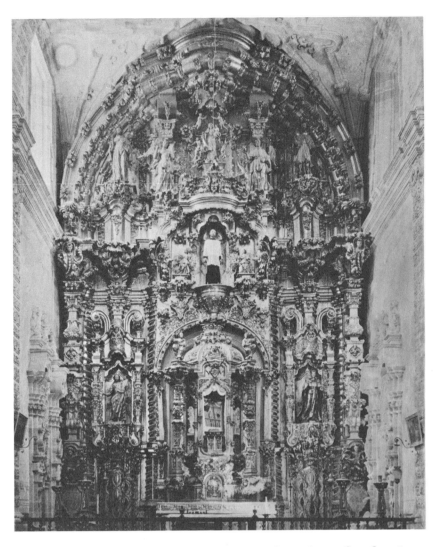

Plate LV-A   La Valenciana, Guanajuato, Guanajuato. San Cayetano, side altar.

of La Valenciana (Plate XIX) is the strict plane that is kept on either side of the central vertical axis. In Santo Domingo de San Cristóbal de las Casas (Plate XXIX) there is a provincial version of what we have seen at Santo Domingo de Oaxaca, but the date is later, and it admits of being covered over with another system of forms, mostly foliations in various kinds of stucco. Of this sort of thing there are variations in all the styles; one learns to read the traditions in different materials, stone, wood carved and gilded, terra cotta, stucco, carved brick, glazed tile. Stucco often is painted, so there are combinations — blue and white, yellow and white (at Antigua) — of forms like this work at San Cristóbal.

But to carry on the increase in fluidity in later styles some new elements, new points of view appear. Primarily there is a change in proportions of most of the classical forms involved. Some new ones are introduced, partly from the point of view of wood, and stucco, and from various places and styles, classical, gothic, Islamic, and mannerist.

The chief of these new forms is the *estipite.* It comes, likely, from Flanders. It appears on furniture, and in interior as well as exterior architecture, and becomes the chief carrier of the styles of the *retablo.* Basically it takes the form of a pilaster and sometimes a column. It has a base. The body is a long inverted pyramid; usually it has a Corinthian capital. Almost always it is broken in the middle by a medallion, either on the outer surfaces or in the body of the form. Its barest essential shape, here actually inverted in the hacienda chapel, Vista Hermosa, Morelos (Plate XXX), shows it in a crude and untypical form. But almost everywhere else, once

Plate LV-B   La Valenciana, Guanajuato, Guanajuato. San Cayetano,
               side altar, upper middle section.

it has come into the style, it is deeply involved with the resources
and duplicated resources of the style.

Going from the little country chapel at Vista Hermosa to the
sagrario of the Metropolitan Church in Mexico City (Plate XXXI), we
can see the richness of the use of the *estipite* in the later development of the style. Here, reading up, there are about seventy elements
on the front plane, duplicated at each side of the pilaster. There are
ten of these *estipites* on each of the exposed sides of the *sagrario.*
With the carved wooden doors, the architraves, the niche panels
and their accessories between the *estipites,* all the details above
the door including the gable make up the statement of the design.

After becoming accustomed to read these forms slowly upward,
and to appreciate the richness of the shadows, one comes to understand the coloristic intention of the whole. It is held back by the
static vertical elements, but on these it seems as something all
about to break out in movement, a hushed, breathless sort of immediacy. It may be seen a little more readily on the gold *retablos,*
the gold altarpieces on the interior, where it actually does move out,
in good rococo examples on which occult balance is common.
Striking in this mode are the side altars in the Dominican Church
in Puebla, where the sculpture is agitated, fluttering as though to
swirl away, within the postulated architectural stability: a visual
paradox. Sometimes these works are breathtaking. They become a
brilliant tour de force in the paradox of movement in the shadows
and the glitter, within rigidly controlled form. This experience is not
an unusual sight. In the porch of the Erechtheum it can be seen in
the six votive figures that support the architrave. In some lights

Plate LV-C   La Valenciana, Guanajuato, Guanajuato. San Cayetano, dome.

the lifted angle of the thigh plane of the figures makes a lighter flash of white, and gives the impression in some momentary lights that the caryatids are slowly walking.

The *sagrario* doors are of great interest (Plate XXXII). The figures of Peter and Paul, the Cross, the Church, the Sword, usual iconographic forms, are carved in high relief on the surface of the doors, and surrounded by high moldings that make the prime pattern of the design. At first glance it may seem that the figures are seen through apertures made by the moldings, and are behind the door. Shadows of the carving contribute to this impression. The device grows when, in interiors, the gold and color used on the great altarpieces enhance this effect. The gold structure seems like a *tabula* of attention; the paintings seen through the apertures seem to be figures in a subjective world, a world of interior space.

At Santa Prisca, Taxco (Plates XXXIII and XXXIV), there are the wonderful niche panel and fine statues, most likely of Peter holding his keys and the central panel of the Baptism. Plate XXXV shows the upper central section of the façade of the former Balvanera chapel of San Francisco. It is white limestone and *tezontle,* the low red-violet volcanic stone used in late Aztec times. Here the break-forth of minor elements of the design, such as the volutes, recalls the tendencies in Islamic art for tangentials, a wayward directioning in the development. But for all the fecund power of this façade, there is one other thing about it that has much interest. Notice the ashlar masonry of the whole *tezontle* gable above the churrigueresque sculpture. See how adventitiously it is built up. Note that the frame around the vacant panel makes an area cut down in violet stone.

Plate LV-D   La Valenciana, Guanajuato, Guanajuato.

See how the framework, though the panels hold no sculpture, takes over the aesthetic situation. Likely there are Islamic implications to be surmised here, since the elaborated framework of the whole façade is an end in itself, and contains almost no iconographic designations, except, of course, the statement of order and power on a structure from the midst of which the *Espiritu Sanctu* pours forth. The deep rich shadows of these forms speak of an immediacy of order.

This is especially clear in the façade of La Compañía, the Church of the Jesuit Order (Plate XXXVI) in Guanajuato. This beautiful building, lifted up a slope, the atrium with its powdery old cedars approached by steep stairways, rises in pale peach-colored stone, almost cerise in tone, over the crass yellow of the buildings around. The sculpture is crisp and clear, with wonderfully defined lights and shadows. There is joy in the upward surge of the release of power in this sculpture that so depends on architecture, and yet is released from it. The ornamental buttress passage, Plate XXXVII, around the tower is a delight of triumph (pure filioque!), and in the niche, on an elaborate console above the window, is one of the elements that make these great sculptural essays a matter of great pleasure, a statue, in a position of arrested movement after the usage of Bernini, in occult balance of lyric movement amidst the strict intellectual organization of all forms around. The powerful gable volutes around the mounting *estipite* here are not to be forgotten.

Perhaps something of this can be surmised in the façade of the Seminario de San Martin at Tepotzotlán (Plate XXXVIII). It has

Plate LVI   The Palace of the Conde de Canal, San Miguel de Allende, Guanajuato. Side doorway.

churrigueresque date, but it is done in a rococo point of view, with the sculpture already sinking into the background plane, the shadows congealing and crowding as the design grows small while the great façade actually seems to expand. Plate XXXIX has remarkable *estipites* and wonderfully elaborated niche panels. But the ornament on the bases of the second stage of *estipites,* around the window over the door, shows a tendency that is innocuous, without distinction and power. The work on this façade is very finely chiseled in fine grain white stone. It is crisp, strong and clear, a tour de force in design and execution.

Santo Domingo de Oaxaca is a notable example of the crypto-collateral churches, and it has elaborate decorations beneath the choir and in the nave itself. Recently the Acción Católica has caused a great new *retablo,* very fine, to be carved to take the place of the one burned in the Revolution. Here, in Plate XL, a view of the cloister looks out over the nave towers and the dome over the choir. In authority and nobility this church and its cloisters and convent buildings remind one of the great conventual buildings in Germany of the eighteenth century. If you turn back now to Plate III, and look at these two side by side, you will see the progress in the architecture of the Mendicant Orders in Mexico from buildings of religious awe and power to buildings that have these characteristics in terms of great art. Now look at Plate I, and you will see this growth clearly.

Not any of the monuments that we have looked at so far can be called exotic. They are in their various ways fully within the tradition. For it is tradition, not freedom from it, that makes for

Plate LVI-A   The Palace of the Conde de Canal, San Miguel
                de Allende, Guanajuato. Side doorway.

invention and its growth into style. For when the artist relies on himself he has nothing; when he relies on himself and tradition, he has everything.

Farther to the north other elements come in. At Saltillo (Plate XLI), one sees an example of a tendency that obtains from about Aguas Calientes to Chihuahua. It may be described as a desire to cover the basic vernacular of *estipites,* columns, niches, entablatures with an added vernacular.

In itself this is not new; you will see tendencies coming out in the astonishing façade at Taxco. In the interiors, when we get to them, this tendency appears very often. But here, rather, and often in the north of Mexico, the vocabulary that is superimposed is stated as an even, all-over pattern. It is common, in various ways, and in various scales, in Peru and Bolivia. The San Lorenzo portal in Potosí, Bolivia will serve as an example of it.[30] It will likely be shown that, although the data, iconographic and conventional, is the usual material, the rhythms and the distribution of lights and shadows have something that may be Indian, may be Islamic, or at least North Andalusian. The visual impact is one of great power.

Much of this work can be produced today. The door here at Saltillo reminds me of the pair of new-carved doors I saw in the cathedral at Chihuahua. One of them bore the arms of that most exalted of men, Piùs XII, with his touching reign talisman, *Opera Justitiae Pax; The Work of Justice is Peace.* Again, we think of a

[30] Pál Kelemen, *Baroque and Rococo in Latin America* (New York: The Macmillan Co., 1951), Plate 127a.

Plate LVII   La Milagrosa, Mexico, Distrito Federal.

recent work, somewhat dry and stiff, the entrance to the Tepeyac chapel at Guadalupe, over the site of the Appearance to Juan Diego (Plate XLII). There is the casual enthronement of Peter and Paul, with Keys and Sword, on the voussoirs of the baroque arch over the main door. And lastly, Merle Wachter's fine trained eye shows us (Plate XLIII) on a private house in Querétaro, *portería* arches, architecture and windows with wonderful passages of eighteenth century bravura with the chisel moving with virtuosity in tracery, shafts, rocaille, *pinjante, faldoncita,* rope, tile, capitals, from faint plateresque indications to deep blacks of later times.

With the Saltillo façade we close the selection of sites that help to illuminate the cause of the Mexican style. For the purposes of this essay the new-classic contributes little to it. It helps to get a long perspective on the problem of the late styles, like the baroque in its phases, if we may look at late styles in other American culture areas.

It has never been pointed out clearly enough that the buildings of the pre-Cortesian tradition are works of sculpture rather than architectural engineering. If you will look at the transverse arch, Ixmiquilpan (Plate IX) or at Plate XLIV, the interior of the Metropolitana, you will see that it is ashlar masonry that makes up the fabric, and that the Spanish traditional prevails in building. One of the interesting things about pre-Cortesian architecture is the degree to which the vernacular of sculpture went through a regular development. It has phases in which can be read some of the history of the growth that can be found in other traditions becoming, as it were, a substitute for ashlar. Plate XLV shows the section of a

Plate LVIII   La Milagrosa, Mexico, Distrito Federal.

façade at Kabah, a Second Maya Empire site that flourished before
the Toltec period in Yucatán. It is made up exactly as were con-
structed some of the monuments that we have been looking at.
The elements are repeated to cover the wall: it is an all-over design
in high relief on rigid planes, made up of separate blocks in its
vernacular aspect, all of which have one or more elements of the
design that is the matter of communication, possibly here the rain-
god Tlaloc, and the protruding nose of the Old Man god. This same
building (Plate XLVI) shows how these blocks are set in rubble,
with rough elongated sides behind the finished designed surface
to hold the block in the wall. Few of them go into the rubble very
far. At Mitla (Plate XLVII) the broken wall shows some tenons that
are longer. But Kabah is late and Mitla is late, and in the centuries
of growth it had not become usual, clearly, to put a tenon from
outer wall to inner wall, to bind them together.

But in all that time, the growth of the way of saying what needs
to be said went on apace, with signs and symbols in sculpture that
usually, at least at Mitla, were covered with fine plaster to take
the red paint that covered these buildings that are all sacerdotal
in character. At Mitla, through the court at the left, you can see
the symbol panels, and the borders of the panels that are symbolic,
the *tepic*, that is the Sacred Hill, the metaphysical elevation, the
universal symbol for contact with the God-world in the cultures of
the New World, and most other places, for that matter.

How little the canons of pre-Cortesian engineering conform to
those of the West can be seen here in this Mitla wall, too. The
sculpture is a skin without much foundation. So when the site starts

103

Plate LIX   La Milagrosa, Mexico, Distrito Federal.

to decay, the sculpture slides off when water weakens walls that are without adequate bases. Along with this, one can see the tons of stone in the cap block that are too heavy for these walls. Commentators on pre-Cortesian "architecture" affect to admire the pathetic skill that can drag these lintels to the top instead of the bottom of the wall. They weigh twenty tons, some of these lintels. Some, we can rationalize, helped to hold the walls in earthquakes. But the values of the aesthetics involved we can scarcely surmise. The church in the background rests on the walls of one of the complexes. The upper part of it is of stone from a quarry nearby. In the middle distance the design of the lintel is carved. The rest of the designs are mosaics. Of these three plates, XLV is the one that interests us most. There is likely an inwardness to the style, as there is an inwardness to the opulent flame and movement of the façade of Santa Prisca and La Santisima that has, like them, as yet to be studied to find more clearly what is to be revealed.

Here, for a few considerations, we can turn from stone to wood. The doorway (Plate XLVIII) will serve as the first example. What we see here in this rich wood treatment is a pair of doors divided into panels that are filled with a design made up of moldings. The molds are jointed at their ends to each other in a variety of angles. The angles are set and arbitrary, and are all available in any carpenter's miter box. Moldings such as these make up a good many of the monuments of plateresque, baroque, churrigueresque and neo-classic style. They can be covered with fine gesso, a smooth plaster, on which may be laid the gold leaf that gives so many of these

Plate LX   La Purísima, Monterrey, Nuevo León.

monuments the highly organized ethereal glitter of color and gold for which they are justly renowned.

At Huejotzingo, on the road to Puebla, in the Franciscan house (Plate XLIX) is this *retablo* that looks in style something like the important *retablo* in the Escorial Church. The paintings are surrounded here by gilded columns and entablatures that remain the structural framework of these altar backgrounds. Given the description of the *estipite,* it is not very difficult to see, at La Valenciana (Plate L), what had happened. Look first at the stone door and enframement in the stone wall. The ornamental pilasters, the duplicated moldings in the impost block as an architrave, the symmetrical balance of the asymmetrical volutes are all in the manner of the late baroque works that we have seen. The gilded woodwork on the altar to the left follows some of these forms. There is the outer *estipite,* then the niche and statue; then the inner *estipite.* A part of the Tabernacle can be seen. The basic forms then are covered with articulation in wood-carving that is added to the parts that can be done with the mitre-cut molding, as can be seen on the right edge of the Tabernacle.

In Plate LI we go to Querétaro country, a town called Salamanca, the Church of San Agustín. Throughout all this region there is a school of the local churrigueresque style, full of verve, a good deal of provincial exuberance, and a variety of rhythms and textures that are anything but Spanish. We are looking at a side altar to the Virgin of Guadalupe. There are the slight pilaster border panels. In the panel itself the light strikes the brilliantly managed console

Plate LXI   El Sagrado Corazón, Colonia del Valle, Mexico, Distrito Federal.

that holds up the kneeling figure. In Plate LII the crown that makes up the canopy over the figure above the Virgin of Guadalupe is a specialty of the region. In the same church, the altar to St. Joseph (Plate LIII) shows some of the detail of the wood carver's bravura. There are a good many Islamic interlaces, like the one over the canopy of Joseph. This same sort of design can be seen even more clearly around the superb console that holds up the group of Christ among the Doctors (Plate LIV). At La Valenciana (Plate LV) we see the exuberance and dramatic variety of this style gloriously set forth. In the first place, the photographs show in the upper regions the effect of light on gold. Here, too, the sculpture is prominent and clear. Often the robes of these figures are old and wonderfully faded. On the shoulders and folds there will be a layer of silver dust. The gold itself will have lost its reds, and survives in tinges of green and black in fading under its own dust. So the bright color aspect of overpowering glitter in gold light from all the reflecting surface, that made a flash of heaven-aspect in power and movement for the priest when he raised the Host, has here after two centuries turned into a dream of gerontic insight, infinitely precious and rare, something to be treasured for all the time that will hold together.

In Mexico today, glorious experiments are being carried out here and there — not least at the Altar of Kings in the Metropolitana — with spotlighting of this sculpture. In San Miguel de Allende, in the Palace of the Conde de Canal, a side door (Plate LVI) shows an example of the range of freedom these styles have afforded. The framework of the styles has nourished an unfettered surge of freedom in many directions. There is scarcely another place in the

106

Plate LXII   La Asunción Cathedral, Oaxaca.

world where such quality and quantity of valuable works of the imagination have so flourished. South India and Ch'ien Lung's China come to mind. The uniqueness of this door can be duplicated many times in Mexico. It is vivid invention in a rich vocabulary of motives. Only the coming of the neo-classic, and the catastrophe of the French Revolution, brought this power in art to a term.

The whole point of this essay is that the arts available to Mexico in the pre-Chichimec regime and in the time after Cortés eventually flowed together to make the art of the viceregal period. After this event there was a century of plunder and neglect that brings us to what Mexico supports today. This can be seen at a series of four churches. The value of these estimations is confined to ecclesiastical structures that form the current architectural statements of a cultural tradition.

It should be pointed out that there have been many post-Revolutionary experiments in secular building and architectural engineering. These have been carried over into the building of churches that proceeds apace in the growth of the cities. La Milagrosa (Plate LVII) shows one of these works in Mexico City in progress. In the ordering of large concrete planes for their own sake you recall the effectiveness of sixteenth century buildings made with mud bricks. If these works produced a simple grandeur it would be enough. But this is what they do not state. The planes are otiose; they obtrude against the whole. This is something that the most flamboyant of churrigueresque face, or *retablo*, or groups of *retablos*, do not do. *They cost the whole nothing, and add much.* Here there is no whole at all. These series of darkened cavities

107

above are something romanesque strove mightily to erase, and to do so eventually, completely. The tradition, here in Mexico, is being broken, gives way to a doing of work that comes not from the forms that belong to the religious culture, but lesser work, infinitely lesser work, from persons. The ego side of creativeness is no place to seek regulating influences that are useful social expressions. Plate LVIII shows this more clearly, and with Plate LIX one sees the frittering, nervous, arbitrary hard lines and forms that also show the raw harshness of concrete, and that are perhaps alien to it. Is not the form to which concrete can lend its greatest usefulness inherent in the parabola?

In Monterrey (Plate LX) at La Purísima there seems to be the best of the post-Revolutionary concrete churches in Mexico. It has great size, and shows the colossal is not the monumental, but of all these buildings, it is closest to the old ways, except for the interior paintings. Least successful, inside and outside, is the Sagrado Corazón (Plate LXI), Colonia del Valle, Mexico City. Nothing farther from an appropriate church for the Marist Order can, I think, be imagined. The statue of the Virgin, gross in that it is larger in scale than the whole high building it surmounts, is brutally stiff as only concrete, dead, hard, and dry, can be stiff. And distance, even great distance, seeing it from way down the avenue, does not soften it at all. Nor is there any virtue in the rough, or artificially roughened, texture of cement. There is no virtue in texture at all, for its own sake, unless one has nothing but texture to state.

Again, the welter of textures in sixteenth and seventeenth century architecture stay in scale; they do not impose themselves on the structure, or on its function. In Mexico one has a feeling that there has been more freedom with concrete, and that the train of events released in the material after the First World War has come to its end. Not in North or South America or in Asia, nor anywhere in Europe, does one feel that the use of it is a success. In fact, until Nervi's time the idea presents itself that no one, designers or engineers, knew what to do with concrete. From this judgment one gladly frees some designers of some bridges. But these Mexican churches of concrete show that the times since 1920 are going fully to realize themselves only in some phase of domestic architecture. For some, a tent for the ego is enough. In the world of Mexican painting comes some encouragement. The great gross giants of the Revolution are giving place to persons of insight, like Jorge González Camarena. In architecture too, there will be a classic return, and signs of it appear in small buildings and some unpretentious domestic architecture.

Now we can turn to the last plate, LXII, the Cathedral of Oaxaca. Glance first at the façade of La Milagrosa, with its conical tower cap and flapping flanges, and see, aside from the Cross, no sign, in Plate LIX, of the expression-language by which the Church teaches. The Church is a teaching institution. It is nothing else. In teaching you are to hold the symbols a matter before the mind and heart and eyes and ears, but especially the eyes, at all times. As any good Leninist will tell you, that is an essential part of the psychology of teaching. When the symbols are gone, the doctrine is gone. And doctrine disappears in the substitution of symbols.

So here at Oaxaca in the Mexico of the eighteenth century, the

Doctrine is at home. There is the high frontal screen between the towers, with its four stages as a teaching device, the old victory arch one over the other, as we saw it on one stage at Acolman. It is sculptured in pale green stone that leaves itself in weathering white in spots and in black lace of long old stains from dripping water, and gold from ferrous oxidation. First, beside the door, are the world's two great teachers, Peter with his Book and Keys; Paul, once more, with his Sword of Salvation. Above is the panel of the Assumption, for the Cathedral, being God's, is also Mary's. Then in the next stage the Eucharist, set out for adoration. Above, recently restored, is the Dove of the Holy Ghost in an aureole. Something to say, something to be believed, something to love.

Place these illustrations side by side. You will see where we are.

If I forget thee, O Jerusalem
Let my right hand forget her cunning!